Guide
to
Confident
Public Speaking

Guide
to
Confident
Public Speaking

James E. Sayer

Nelson-Hall nh Chicago

LIBRARY OF CONGRESS CATALOGING IN PUBLICATION DATA

Sayer, James E.
  Guide to confident public speaking.

  Includes bibliographical references and index.
  1. Public speaking. I. Title.
PN4121.S2776 1983   808.5′1   82-8080
ISBN 0-88229-734-1 (cloth) AACR2
ISBN 0-88229-808-9 (paper)

Manufactured in the United States of America

10 9 8 7 6 5 4 3 2 1

The paper in this book is pH neutral (acid-free).

*To those who would like to speak in public
and enjoy it.*

Contents

1

Have You Ever Been Afraid?

"I thought I was going to die. My hands and legs shook so much I thought I'd fall over. I was scared to death."

"My stomach felt like a big knot, and I could feel the perspiration rolling down my face. I wished the ground would open up and swallow me—I wanted to be anywhere but there."

"I was okay until I tried to start. Then, and I know this sounds weird, I swear that my tongue was at least twice its normal size. I couldn't swallow, and I couldn't breathe. I opened my mouth, but nothing came out. It was the most helpless feeling I've ever had."

Those statements were not made by people facing life-or-death situations, nor by people appearing on a televised quiz show. No, they were made by ordinary people who were called upon to speak in public. Their "enemy" was not a mugger with a knife or a competitor trying to win thousands of dollars. Their only enemy was fear—their fear of public speaking overwhelmed and incapacitated them.

Have you ever felt like that? Have you ever been afraid to speak in public? If so, then this book is for you and for many other people who do not like to speak in public and who actively avoid situations where they might be called upon someday to make a speech.[1]

1

This book is not going to tell you that your fear is unreal or that you ought to be ashamed of it. You know that the fear is real, so real that it can paralyze speakers and make them virtually unable to speak. What this book will do is show you how your fear can be overcome. The result is glorious: public speaking may prove to be one of the most exciting and enjoyable experiences of your life.

If I sound like some type of public speaking zealot, I should, because I am one. I have found that speaking in public is exhilarating and fun. To control an audience, to have them react the way you want them to, is most satisfying, and that satisfaction need not be limited to a select few. Everyone can share that feeling, and this book is written so that you may experience the same exhilaration and enjoyment that I feel when I speak in public.

PUBLIC SPEAKERS ARE MADE, NOT BORN

A fairly common misconception says that effective public speakers—those people who please audiences and who do not appear frightened at having to present a speech—are gifted with some sort of "knack" or God-given ability that the rest of us do not possess. According to this theory, some people have been divinely predestined to be able to speak well, and they sprang forth from their cradles with soul-stirring orations on their lips. While that view might make for an interesting Hollywood movie on the life of Daniel Webster or some other famous speaker of the past, it has nothing to do with the truth. Effective public speakers were not and are not anointed at birth. Effective public speakers are made, not born—everyone, barring severe mental or physical disorders, may become an effective public speaker. Maybe you think that this statement does not apply to you; that you could never become an effective speaker or enjoy speaking to an audience. It is important for you to realize that saying or believing such things does not make them true. As we'll discuss later in this chapter, you may be your own worst enemy.[2] You may be the one blocking your growth as an effective public communicator. For now, all I ask you to do is to approach public speaking with an open mind—to overcome the belief that some people have the innate ability to speak well and others do not. You have the capabilities to be an effective public speaker and to enjoy each public speaking experience. All you have to do is be open to developing those capabilities you already possess.

STAGEFRIGHT IS NATURAL

"I really admire Ruth. When she got up in front of the PTO, she was so cool that you could see she wasn't nervous. I wish I could do it. Why isn't Ruth scared?"

Have you ever made or heard a comment about someone who seemed to be "cool as a cucumber" while speaking? Have you ever thought that such a person must have "nerves of steel" to be able to speak without shaking or pacing nervously?

Much like the myth concerning public speaking ability, a corollary myth says that some people are not scared to speak in public. In fact, everyone is affected by stagefright to some degree in a public speaking situation. Even the most experienced and skilled speakers feel the pangs of stagefright. Stagefright is never completely eliminated, but it can be overcome.[3]

In dealing with stagefright, the only substantial difference between you and more experienced public speakers is that they have had more experience in handling stagefright. They expect to feel some pangs of fear and are prepared to overcome it. Perhaps they accomplish that task so well that you cannot detect even the slightest trace of concern on their parts, but stagefright is present even for the most polished and urbane speaker you can imagine. Stagefright is something you must expect, and with preparation and practice, stagefright will be relatively easy for you to overcome.

Do you remember what it was like when you learned to ride a bicycle? The first few times you tried to ride without training wheels, you probably fell on your nose. However, each time you climbed on that bike and began to pedal, you went just a bit farther than before—then you fell again. It was a time of combined frustration and determination, but you were going to ride that bike no matter how many times you fell off. Finally you mounted your bike, and although you wobbled like a cheap table, you did not fall. You had learned to ride a bicycle—one of your earliest childhood victories and one of the sweetest moments in your lifetime. What I want you to do is to bring that same sense of determination, that same dogged commitment to success, to public speaking. If you will risk falling on your nose in front of an audience, then you have what it takes to be an effective public speaker. If you have the determination to succeed, then you will succeed—just as you learned to ride that bike many years ago.

One of the most effective and impressive public speakers of the twentieth century was Bishop Fulton J. Sheen, a man who possessed a most captivating speaking delivery. Was he always such a fine speaker? Sheen was far from it. As a young man, he was so poor a speaker that his teachers suggested he take public speaking courses to become at least tolerable. Fighting severe stagefright and shyness, Bishop Sheen applied himself and became one of the most revered speakers in American history.

Will you ever totally eliminate stagefright? No, you will always feel some degree of nervousness, especially when speaking before a strange group for the first time. Even a man about to deliver his millionth speech would feel some stagefright. You will learn how to overcome your fear and how to make stagefright actually work for you. The only difference between you and that man about to deliver his millionth speech is experience; there are no mysterious secrets. What that man can do now, you will be able to do soon.[4]

STAGEFRIGHT IS HELPFUL

Stagefright is helpful? When you saw that heading you might have asked yourself, "Who does he think he's kidding? I've had stagefright and all it did was scare the hell out of me! Stagefright is helpful???"

Yes, believe it or not, stagefright can be helpful. All of us have been bored by the monotonous dronings of speakers who challenge our abilities to stay awake. These speakers ought to be termed "Geritol speakers," because they appear to need a strong dose of that elixir to put some life into their speaking style. Nothing can be deadlier to the effectiveness of a speech than a speaker who arouses boredom. The presence of a small degree of stagefright can help a speaker reduce the tendency to bore an audience.

Much as an athlete feels when facing a supreme competitive challenge, a speaker may feel "charged up" by stagefright. That fear of failure so natural to everyone serves to charge us up, to put us on our toes, and to make us dynamic and interesting speakers. Stagefright actually performs a great service for us, exciting us to perform to maximum potential and to seem more alive and effective on stage.

Stagefright gets our blood pumping and our minds working; we function at a greatly accelerated pace. This extra boost of energy then is translated into our speaking manner, helping us to be outgoing and dynamic. Fear causes tension, and this tension is released through extra energy in our bodies. This energy, in turn, serves to improve our speaking and the impact we have upon our audiences.

Stagefright itself is nothing to fear; it should be welcomed because of the beneficial impact it has upon our speaking potential. Stagefright can be one of the most useful tools in the speaker's kit, as it heightens the dynamism and vitality that all public speakers need to exhibit. In fact, were you ever to face a strange audience for the first time without having some degree of stagefright, then you would have a reason to be afraid, because you would lack that dynamic tension which helps you to speak effectively.

YOUR OWN WORST ENEMY IS YOURSELF

Many people fear giving a public speech because they expect the worst to happen. While it is impossible to catalogue all such fears, the following list highlights some of the major concerns:

- forgetting part or all of the speech; having to stand in front of a jeering audience while trying to remember "what comes next"
- tripping or falling down while speaking, knocking over the podium, and other such klutzy disasters
- becoming ill while speaking or being unable to control such involuntary actions as giggling and stammering
- having the audience laugh at what the speaker considers to be a serious point; having the audience not laugh at what the speaker thought would be funny
- mispronouncing words or butchering the language to the point of audience hilarity[5]

Such a list could be endless, but it demonstrates that speakers have feared practically every potential disaster. You have feared similar tragedies.

You must realize that fear emphasizes the bizarre, the infrequent, the unlikely. The probability that you would knock over the podium is so small that it could not be measured. In the past decade or so, I have seen thousands of speeches and have delivered several hundred myself. On all those occasions, only once have I seen the podium knocked over, and I happened to pull that trick myself. What did I do? I kept speaking, did not let it bother me, and the audience wasn't affected by my klutziness one iota.

You see, the biggest problem you face as a speaker is the *expectation of failure,* the belief that something will go wrong —that something *has* to go wrong. You may be one of those people who say, "I just know that this speech isn't going to be any good. The audience won't like it. They'll be bored. After all, I'm not interesting, I haven't got anything to say. What have I gotten myself into?" Such intrapersonal fear is not justified and serves only to make things more difficult for you. Instead of working to help, such thoughts are debilitating and psychologically depressing. No wonder so many people face public speaking the way a condemned man faces the gallows.

You can change your negative outlook. Instead of "psyching" yourself out, you should "psych" yourself up. After all, you have been selected to make the speech because others have faith in you. Why demonstrate so little faith in yourself? When you speak, you are in control, you are the expert. Instead of approaching the podium fearfully, you ought to walk with confidence and pride, because you will be the center of attention, you will be the person to whom everyone listens. Instead of expecting failure, expect success. Emphasize your strong points, and work to eliminate your weak ones. If you will approach each speaking situation in a positive state of mind, you will succeed—it's that simple.

One more point should be made concerning speaker expectations and perceptions: The person who has the worst or most slanted perception of what takes place during a speech is the speaker. Because all energies are devoted to the presentation of the speech, heightened by the presence of stagefright, the speaker tends to be aware of everything and to blow it out of proportion. Thus, small nervous shaking in the arms or legs feels, to the speaker, like the gigantic gyrations of a jack-in-the-box. Perspiration on the nose or over the upper lip feels like a river of water cascading down the face. Those feelings and perceptions are quite natural, heightened by your presence in the spotlight. However, they are not noticeable to your audience. Even though you may feel that you are going to shake yourself out of your shoes, your audience will not see your shaking, nor will they see you sweat. In fact, the only nervous mannerism that any audience will perceive is that of the shaking or tremulous voice, and that weakness can be eliminated by careful prespeech preparation and practice. In truth, the speaker has the worst perception of what is going on and invariably sees the worst, though the audience does not. The worst enemy you face is yourself, and that knowledge will help you to overcome your fear of public speaking.

OTHERS WANT YOU TO SUCCEED

Most stagefright is audience-centered, meaning that the speaker fears the reactions of the audience. Often, the audience is seen as the enemy, a group of people who are out to "get" the speaker. Truthfully, this perception is totally incorrect, much like most other perceptions that beginning speakers have concerning public speaking.

Actually, the members of the audience want you to do well; they want you to succeed. They have no desire for you to fail; they will pull for you all the way through your presentation. Two major reasons appear to explain this supportive audience posture.

First, every member of the audience has been placed in the position occupied by the speaker; at some time, each one has been asked to present a speech and has felt the qualms and fears you feel. Thus, they will be supportive, because they know what you are going through. They know that you have butterflies in your stomach; they know every fear or self-doubt that you have experienced. Because of their own experiences, the audience will be sympathetic to you and your situation. When you are a member of an audience, how do you feel? Are you sympathetic to the speaker? Do you hope that the speech goes well? Of course you do, and every member of your audience will feel the same way towards you. You should feel a great deal of encouragement and support from the audience's positive orientation.

A second reason for audience support might seem more selfish. No one likes to sit through a boring or botched speech. People will want your speech to go well so that they will not have to endure a long-suffering presentation. A well-organized and well-presented public speech is a thing of beauty and enjoyment for the audience. Because of that fact, the audience will want you to do well so that they may be able to enjoy your public speech.

Remember, the audience is not your enemy; the audience is

not out to "get" you. On the contrary, the audience will prove to be supportive. Your biggest enemy is not your audience but yourself and your own negative expectations and perceptions.

WHAT YOU SHOULD DO AND NOT DO

This chapter will conclude by discussing some ways for you to overcome stagefright, as well as several other things you ought to avoid. First, we will look at the constructive side:

1. Nothing overcomes stagefright better than ample pre-speech preparation and practice. You must spend a reasonable amount of time researching, writing, organizing, and practicing the delivery of your speech. If you are thoroughly prepared, even the most severe case of the jitters will not overwhelm you. Instead, your prespeech preparation and practice will see you through. Your mouth will open and your well-prepared speech will roll out, sometimes to your surprise and amazement. The key word, then, is *practice.*

2. You need to realize that your audience is on your side, pulling for you to do well. Your audience should be seen not as a stumbling block, but as your friends. You should have a positive attitude towards your audience before you speak.

3. Recognize that the disasters you expect to befall you simply will not happen. The earth will not stop rotating on its axis when you approach the speaker's podium. In addition, even if something does go awry (you mispronounce a word; you don't say something exactly the way you planned to say it), the audience will not be aware of it.

4. Realize that your biggest problem is internal: your own negative expectations. You must believe in yourself. A positive, confident attitude, when coupled with adequate preparation and practice, leads to effective public speaking.

5. Finally, recognize that you are not alone in your fears. Every public speaker—past, present, and future—has the jit-ters. The president of the United States is nervous before the presentation of the State of the Union address; a teacher is

nervous before the first lecture of the term. Patrick Henry had stagefright and so did Daniel Webster. That puts you in pretty good company, and you will overcome stagefright just as they did.

Besides concentrating upon the above-noted five items, you will find that you will be better able to handle stagefright *if you do not do the following:*

1. You should not put yourself through the intense psychological process of trying to convince yourself that you will not be nervous by saying over and over, "I won't be nervous. I won't be nervous. I won't be nervous." Of course you will be nervous. Not only is nervousness to be expected, but it pays great dividends in creating a dynamic and interesting speaking style. You might wish to use deep-breathing and relaxing exercises to calm you, but trying to persuade yourself that you will not be nervous is absurd and counterproductive.

2. Contrary to some advice you might hear, you should not approach a public speaking situation as if you were speaking to yourself. You would never place yourself behind a podium if you intended only to speak to yourself. That would look and feel ridiculous. You are in a public speaking situation to have your thoughts consumed by other people, not to speak to yourself. Besides, you will know you are not simply speaking to yourself the moment you see the faces of your audience.

3. You should not attempt to reduce nervousness by avoiding eye contact with your audience. Some speakers refuse to look at their audience, preferring to look over the tops of the audience members' heads. As is discussed in chapters 2 and 6, it is essential that you have direct eye contact with your audience for feedback and effective delivery. Refusing to have eye contact only irritates the audience and does nothing to alleviate stagefright.

4. Finally, you should not memorize your speeches. Quite simply, a memorized speech is a bomb waiting to explode, because the least bit of disruption or distraction will cause such

speakers to forget "what comes next" as they lose their train of thought. A speaker must be able to make changes, to handle the unexpected, and a memorized speech does not allow the speaker that necessary flexibility. It is somewhat seductive to believe that a memorized speech overcomes stagefright because the speaker does not have to think, but an effective speaker must think while speaking. Stagefright is only concealed by memorization rather than overcome.

You are not alone in feeling the pangs of stagefright. Everyone has felt such fear. But you can and will overcome stagefright—if you are willing to allow yourself some time and experience. Have you ever been afraid? Of course you have, and so have I, but now is the time to overcome that fear and to enjoy public speaking!

Notes

Chapter 1

Have You Ever Been Afraid?

1. All of us know many people who have an intense fear of speaking in public. The 1977 *Book of Lists* reported the results of a national survey which revealed that hundreds of people feared having to give a speech more than they feared dying.

2. One of the most extensively studied communication variables has been that of stagefright (and its correlative terms *communication anxiety* and *communication apprehension*). These studies indicate that most stagefright is self-induced, literally making the speaker the cause of the anxiety.

3. I would further add that a failure to feel even a tinge of stagefright when preparing to speak before a strange audience might indicate a physiological dysfunction on your part. It is both psychologically and physiologically natural to feel some degree of nervousness.

4. Not too long from now, you will be amazed that you ever feared speaking in public. The more speaking experience you get, the better you will be.

5. A most comprehensive list of such fears is provided by Janet Stone and Jane Bachner, *Speaking Up* (New York: McGraw-Hill, 1977), p. 35.

2

What Happens When You Communicate

QUESTION: What takes place when you communicate with someone else?

ANSWER: It's really very simple. One person says something and the other person just listens.

QUESTION: Then why do misunderstandings occur? If it's so simple, why don't we easily understand each other all the time?

ANSWER: Because sometimes we don't use the right word to say something. If we were very careful in choosing words, we would not have any communication problems.

The foregoing dialogue clearly illustrates the most common misconception about communication—that it is a simple thing. One person talks and the next person listens is often the street definition of oral communication.

If communication between people were that easy, then there would be no need for this book, or for any book dealing with human communication. If communication were easy, there would be no need for courses in public speaking, for such organized groups as Toastmasters International, or for many professional people with the title of "communication consultant." If communication were easy, you would never feel the pangs of stagefright.

Communication is never that simple. The transmission of information between people involves much more than having one person speak while another person listens, and improving our daily communication encounters requires more than being very careful in choosing words. Any process which involves the interaction of people is complex, because people cannot easily be pegged in neat descriptive containers (as every political leader has learned since time began).

Since no two people are exactly alike, the nature of communication varies with the individuals involved. Some people like to hear funny stories from a speaker, while other people feel insulted when a speaker employs such humor. Some people can understand even the most disorganized speech imaginable, while others have to be led A-B-C through the simplest discourse. An old Prudential Insurance Company advertisement several years ago proclaimed, "There's nobody else exactly like you," and that statement is correct. There is no one just like you, me, or anyone else. The differences make human communication both difficult and challenging.[1]

THE COMMUNICATION TRANSACTION

It is not uncommon to hear communication scholars describe the nature of communication as a "process," meaning that a number of factors go through a constant state of change during any communication encounter. Even the simplest dialogue involves a number of complex variables.

Perhaps the most efficient way to explain the dynamic nature of the communication process is to contrast it with something unlike it. Perhaps you enjoy going to the race track to see the horses run. If you went to the Kentucky Derby, you could film a race for later viewing at home. As you watched the replay of that race, you could examine your film frame by frame until the lead horse's nose crossed the finish line, and at that exact point you could proclaim with certainty which horse had won the Kentucky Derby. Similarly, you could watch an instant replay of a field goal attempt in a football game, and the moment the ball sailed over the crossbar between the uprights you could say that the field goal attempt had been successful. You cannot do the same type of analysis with human communication.

Were I to film your conversation with a neighbor or your speech before a group, I could not pull one frame from my film and exclaim, "That is communication," because communication was taking place both before and after that frame. You send and receive messages all the time, as do the members of your audience. There is no clear division between points where communication exists and where it does not. The human communication process is so dynamic and all-encompassing that there is great truth to the saying, You cannot *not* communicate.

To clarify the operation of factors in a communication transaction, we will look briefly at the major components of the communication process: source, message, channel, receiver.[2]

The S-M-C-R Factors

Figure 2.1 provides a simple way to examine the factors involved in the human communication process. The four factors placed in the middle of the diagram (source, message, channel, receiver) are the foundations of all communication types, both oral and written. All four factors are present in every communication transaction.

The *source* is that individual who initiates the communication encounter ("Good morning, Fred. You're looking really sharp today!"). The source serves as the stimulus for everything that follows.

The *message* involves the language and the meanings conveyed by the source. Later in this chapter, we will note that not all messages are verbalized; meanings may also be transmitted through body language and vocal inflections.

The *channel* is the medium by which the message is sent from the source to the listener(s). In a public lecture, the channel

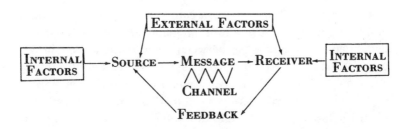

Fig. 2.1 The Communication Transaction

would be the air that carries sound from the speaker to the ears of the audience. Other channels include television, radio, and telephone.

The *receiver* gets the message from the source. The receiver may be one person, as in an informal conversation, or it may be an audience at a more formalized public speaking setting.

These four components must be present in all types of communicative encounters—formal and informal, large and small, planned and extemporaneous. In written communication, the four elements could be analyzed as follows: source (writer), message, channel (paper upon which words are written), and receiver (reader).

In public speaking settings, there will also be another factor of utmost importance: *feedback.* You will note on the communication transaction diagram that feedback appears to flow from the receiver to the source. One tremendous advantage you will have as a speaker is that your audience will give you feedback throughout your presentation, allowing you to know how your audience sees you and your message. This feedback is important, because it tells you if your speech is going well or if you might need to make some modifications to enhance clarity, attentiveness, and interest. Several examples will demonstrate the importance of this receiver-to-source information flow.

John spoke before a group at the weekly meeting of the Ringers Club. Several minutes into his presentation, John noticed that some members of the audience were stifling yawns, shifting about in their seats, and occasionally shaking their heads as if trying to stay awake. "I must be boring them," thought John, "I'd better tell my favorite joke to win back their attention and interest."

Marsha served as the chairperson of the local United Way Campaign. Wanting to contact as many people as possible to solicit contributions, she persuaded the town's television station manager to give her ten minutes free air time to broadcast an appeal for funds.

Despite her sincere efforts, Marsha's message rambled, was poorly organized, and was generally very difficult to follow. Viewers turned off their tv sets, and Marsha's message was beamed to a nonviewing public.

Felix decided to spend part of his summer vacation in Hawaii, using money he had set aside during the past three years. He thought that Marty might like to go with him, so he wrote Marty a letter, asking him to accompany him on his paradise vacation. When Marty didn't write back, Felix decided to take the trip alone and made all the necessary travel arrangements. On the morning of his departure, Felix received a brief note from Marty: "Trip idea really sounds great! When do we go?"

The significance of immediate feedback should be clear to you after reading these three examples. In the first example, audience feedback in a public speaking situation alerted John to the need for recapturing the attention and interest of his audience. However, in the other two examples, the sources of the message (Marsha and Felix) did not have access to immediate feedback, and as a result their communication efforts suffered. Marsha could not see her television audience, so she did not know until it was too late that her poor presentation caused her message to be turned off. Similarly, Felix did not receive a response from Marty until it was too late to plan a Hawaiian trip for both of them. Only John had the advantage of the instantaneous feedback inherent in the public speaking setting, and he was bright enough to seize this advantage.

Public speakers should not fear their audiences, because audience feedback lets them know how they and their message are coming across to the audience. Feedback serves as the window to audience reactions, giving the speaker a chance to see how to improve the impact of later speeches.

External Stimuli

Human communication still might be considered relatively simple if it were made up only of those S-M-C-R factors, plus feedback. However, each of those factors is comprised of many other elements, adding another layer of complexity.

For example, imagine yourself in a public speaking situation acting as the source of a message. Are you simple? Are you easy to comprehend? Are you but a one-dimensional character? Of course not—nobody is, except perhaps a cartoon character. No, you are a complex mixture of goals, desires, motivations, and contradictions. That complexity makes human psychology an interesting subject—there is so much to study.

Everything that combines to make you who you are affects your role as the source of human communication. Your personality often determines with whom you will communicate and how, and your personality affects the success or failure of your various communication efforts. Your heredity, environment, education, vocabulary, and race or ethnic culture also have impacts upon communication.

The total composite of your existence plays a large role in determining the answers to these questions:

1. What is your attitude toward speaking? Do you enjoy speaking to others?

2. What do you like to speak about? What topics or issues do you prefer to avoid?

3. When do you like to speak? Under what circumstances do you seldom choose to speak?

4. To whom do you like to speak, and to whom do you avoid speaking?

Not only psychological factors affect your speaking opportunities and performances; specific environmental factors also affect your speaking efforts. Have you ever had a "bad day?" Perhaps you overslept and got off to a late start. Your car had a flat tire, and, in an effort to make up for lost time, you were ticketed for speeding. All of us have had days like that, and some of us have had weeks like that. Such experiences affect how you communicate.

After having one of those disaster-after-disaster experiences, you might have this type of communicative interchange:

YOU: (Much mumbling and grumbling)
OTHER: "Hey, buddy, how's it going? Isn't it a great day?!"
YOU: "Will you stop that drivel? When did you become a meteorologist and begin giving pronouncements about the weather?"
OTHER: "What'd I do? What'd I do???"
YOU: (Much mumbling and grumbling)

Your current physical and emotional states affect your communication with others. Whether you are happy, sad, angry, mellow, ill, or agitated will have a significant impact upon you as a speaker. Moreover, because your audience is composed of people who are just as complex as you, audience reactions to your message will be affected by the external stimuli pertinent to those people. You may have heard the old public speakers' saw, No two audiences are alike—which is true, but to which you should add that no two speakers are alike, either. Since the many external stimuli are different for each person (even the same stimulus may affect people differently), this variable of external forces will be of great significance to all your human communication experiences, both private and public.

Internal Stimuli

The complexity of human communication is increased by the presence of internal stimuli, those factors that are peculiar to your specific speaking situation at the moment. Because you react differently to different people and under differing speaking situations, no two communication encounters are exactly alike.

For example, you are affected by the reason for communicating,[3] why you have chosen to communicate in the first place. Consider the significant differences between the following reasons for speaking to someone:

- An acquaintance stops you on the street and asks how you are.
- You decide to approach your boss to ask for a raise.
- You decide to tell your wife or husband that you want a divorce.
- You approach your neighbor to ask that he quiet his barking dog.
- You order a banana split at the local ice cream store.

In some instances, you engage in relatively unimportant "ritualistic" communication ("Hey, Fred, How's it going?") that means little to you and causes no anxiety. In other circumstances, such as asking your boss for a raise, you are quite anxious about that outcome of your communication encounter. The very nature of the speaking situation affects your thoughts, feelings, and behavior.

In all situations, your image plays an important part in how you see yourself ("I am this person's superior;" "I am this person's inferior") and in how you believe that the other person or persons see you ("I'm sure he thinks I'm a nerd."). You also make judgments about the other person's intelligence, self-worth, value in direct relation to you, and other factors.

It is important to remember that no one in a communication situation, regardless of that situation's formality or informality, enters that situation with a blank slate. All of us have beliefs about ourselves and about others, even about people we have never met before. By stereotyping and making quick judgments based on appearances, we decide whether someone is trustworthy, sincere, or credible, and each of these lightning-fast decisions affects the outcome of a communication encounter.

In a public speaking situation, the success of your speech will be affected greatly by

1. how you see yourself vis-à-vis the speaking situation
2. how you see yourself vis-à-vis your audience
3. how you believe your audience sees your topic
4. how you believe your audience sees you
5. how you hope your audience will see you and your topic during and after your speech

Your decisions about what to say and how to say it are based upon the answers you supply to the five questions above.

In effect, every word you utter within a speech is a result of an internal dialogue that may go something like this: *I want to get my audience to contribute to the United Way, but I just can't walk out and say, "Please give to the United Way." They have to have a reason for donating money, considering inflation and all that. I guess I could show that the United Way needs money and let them draw the conclusion that contributions are necessary. But many people might think I was only describing a situation and not really asking for donations.*

I guess what I'd better do is both explain the financial plight of the United Way and directly ask for their help. That way, I can both justify my request and, at the same time, make sure that my request is understood.

That process of intrapersonal communication takes only a few seconds, and all of us do it many times each day in our various communication encounters. We decide what we want (aspiration), and then we haggle with ourselves about how to say it and about how our message will be interpreted. The complexities of the human communication transaction clearly show that communication involves much more than having "one person speak while another person listens."

THE NATURE OF LANGUAGE

Each individual must deal and communicate with many other people every day. We come into contact with a large number of people with whom we must work, co-operate, and communicate for a variety of reasons. To carry out these communication efforts, we must master the use of language in the conceptualization, transmission, and evaluation of our own and others' thoughts and ideas. Words serve as our tools as we transfer messages from source to receiver and back again.

Although words serve to transmit messages, the actual words themselves do not possess fixed meanings. The meanings that we ascribe to words are purely arbitrary, social conventions that represent the majority's view as to what each word means. To illustrate this point, consider the word *house*. A simple word, isn't it? Certainly, there should be no confusion as to what is meant.

However—and this is important in understanding the nature of language—*what the source had in mind when transmitting the message may not be the same message transferred to the receiver.* In the illustration above, the source may have been thinking of an older, two-story house, while the receiver pictured a new, rambling suburban ranch house instead. Therefore, although both the source and the receiver agreed upon the structure of the message—they both recognized the five-letter word *house*—the same word conjured up two different meanings for the people involved in the communicative interchange. Future source references to this house would not mesh well with the receiver's conceptualization of *house*.

Words do not always convey the same meanings to people. Because each of us has different life experiences and expectations, our language, and the meanings we attach to our language, will vary dramatically from one person to another. Thus, the meanings that we give to words, especially those found in such reference aids as dictionaries, are selected arbitrarily. Such meanings are no more than the generally accepted meanings within a particular culture.

Language, therefore, involves nothing more than abstract symbols, internal images and meanings that we want to communicate to other people. The arbitrariness of language is demonstrated quite easily by considering the actual words used. For example, no divine mandate has required that we call a four-legged member of the feline family a cat instead of a telephone. We could have labeled a chair a house, a boy a car, or a bucket a hose. The words employed are quite arbitrary; the importance of language lies not in the arbitrary definition of words (denotation) but in the individualized meanings that we give to them (connotation).

To better illustrate the point that "true meanings" are in us and not in the words themselves, take a pen or pencil and some paper and write a brief definition of each of the words that follow. Next, give the same list of words to another person, have that person define them, and then compare your definitions. You will find that almost every word has conjured up different, and sometimes contradictory, meanings.

- Intellectual
- Socialist
- Liberal
- Politician
- Conservative
- Republican
- Democrat
- Democracy
- Freedom
- Truth

This simple comparison of your personal definitions with those of another clearly indicates that the operational definitions of words—that is, how we actually use them and react to them—are not inherent. Meanings are not in words but in the people who use them.[4] In short, when someone asks you "What do you mean?" you will never be able to state exactly what you had in mind.

The ambiguity and impreciseness of language is best seen by considering how language is used in the overall human communication process via the process of symbolization. There are three main factors within the symbolization process, and each deserves individual analysis.

Referents

Whenever we speak, we refer to specific ideas, concepts, matters, objects, or events. If I were to talk to you about a tree, the tree itself would be considered the referent in our communicative interchange, because that object is the subject of our discussion. Similarly, were we to talk about freedom, freedom would be the referent. Referents can be intangible ideas as well as material objects.

Symbols

In deciding to talk or write about a particular referent, we choose to transfer something from ourselves to others. Oral and written communication depends upon language to serve as the primary tool of message transmission. We symbolize our referents through the use of language.

The use of symbols is best observed when dealing with abstract or intangible referents such as freedom. *Freedom* is a word that people tend to use with little precision. We use it to describe personal actions, academic actions, governmental actions, and mental processes. Politicians, especially during reelection campaigns, have a penchant for overusing this word in descriptions and justifications for all sorts of actions and proposed programs. What, then, is this word *freedom*?

It is sufficient for our purposes to realize that the word *freedom* is but a linguistic symbol that stands for a general, somewhat vague concept that is the referent within this communicative interchange. The word *freedom* itself is nothing more than the symbol for the generalized referent. Symbols are a shorthand way of representing the referent, whether the referent be of a tangible or intangible nature.

Images

Having considered the existence of referents and symbols, we can finally turn our attention to the third component of the symbolization process: the creation of images. The difficulty of image creation relates directly to the concept of meaning explored earlier. Since words (symbols) do not possess static, inherent meanings that are true for all people at all times, there can be many possible interpretations or meanings (images) for every symbol. We are so much involved with our language that we literally become emotionally interwoven with the symbols that serve only as representatives for referents. *Freedom* is but a symbol of an intangible referent, but because we live within a society that places so much emphasis upon this concept, *freedom* becomes much more than a cold symbolic representation. *Freedom* takes on important emotionalized loadings that can affect our existence and our everyday lives. Wars are fought, people are injured, entire civilizations are ravaged for the sake of achieving or maintaining freedom, despite the fact that the symbol means many different things to people.

Therefore, in considering an overall view of the process of symbolization, it is important to realize that your language usage is inherently going to be nonspecific, that you will never be able to transfer the meaning of your message to your receiver exactly as you wish. Instead, you will be trying to use language to create images in your audience's minds that will be consistent with the images within your own mind that underlie your message. Good language, then, is language use that tends to create the effect desired by the source—language that transfers consistent images of symbol and referent from the source to the receiver.

NONVERBAL COMMUNICATION

We conclude our brief examination of the complex components of the human communication process by considering an area that has come under increasing study during the past ten years—nonverbal communication.[5]

We learn early in life that a speaker's message is not contained entirely within the words chosen. Realizing that language is imprecise and that meaning shifts from one person's interpretation to another, we look for other clues to another's message. Often, we turn to various nonverbal stimuli to help provide this other dimension of meaning.

In human communication, we use nonverbal stimuli to fill those gaps left by the structure of language. The speaker's tone of voice influences our assessment of both the meaning and intent of the message; we often judge sincerity or trustworthiness in terms of eye contact or lack of it, and we interpret a speaker's bodily movements and posture as signs of friendliness or hostility. In short, we use nonverbal stimuli such as vocal tone, eye contact, and posture to supplement the vague and incomplete meanings transmitted via language. Nonverbal communication cues complete the human communication process.

Physical Elements

In direct, personal communication settings, the most obvious nonverbal factor is the other person's face. You observe the other person's facial expressions, and you make judgments based upon those facial expressions. Facial expressions are among the most important of all nonverbal stimuli.

If you were speaking to a group of people and you noted that many of your audience members were scowling, you would probably believe that they disagreed with your message. Despite the fact that no one said a word to you, a message was definitely sent from listener to speaker, and you would try to do something to remove those negative expressions. Facial expressions often provide us with a great deal of unspoken information about audience reaction to our message, and a speaker would be wise to take advantage of this additional information.

Similarly, facial expression is important when you are listening and not speaking. If the speaker grins during a speech, or if the face is tightly drawn into a grimace, you will conjure up varied reactions towards the message and the speaker. We often hear that someone appeared to be cocky during a speech, an attribute often ascribed because of facial expression. If the speaker appears smug, disinterested in his audience, or belligerent, we may "turn the speaker off" because of the attitude conveyed by facial movements and not because of the exact words that have been uttered.

Besides general facial expression, the eyes are critically important in nonverbal communication. Specifically, eye contact between individuals in a communicative interchange plays a significant role in the beginning, continuing, and ending of the communication process. Studies have indicated that eye contact with another person generally fills three main functions: it opens the channels of communication, provides information about people and their messages, and constantly regulates, monitors and eventually concludes communication.

In normal situations, you do not simply approach people and begin to speak. Instead, you first try to establish the presence of communicative capability; that is, whether the other person is willing to receive what you wish to say. Thus, eye contact is used to open communication channels whereby you will "have the floor" to speak. Once you have gained the other's eye contact, there is implicit agreement that you may speak. Conversely, when the other's eye contact drifts away towards another person or object, you have been told nonverbally that your message is no longer of interest or importance. In effect, the lines of communication have been closed and your message no longer has an attentive audience.

For some reason, probably due to natural nervousness and initial stage fright, many speakers find it quite difficult to establish and maintain direct eye contact with their audiences. Often they fear that they will not be able to withstand "all those eyes looking at me." However, you need to realize that such direct eye contact is crucial in opening the lines of communication between yourself and your audience, and you should strive to maintain this direct eye contact throughout each speech. There is no shortcut to effective eye contact; there are no tricks to be taught. Certainly, the old elementary school advice that you should simply look over the tops of the heads of your audience does not hold water. The listener knows when the speaker is looking at the back of the room. Eye contact serves to open communication channels, and you should constantly use this excellent communicative device.

We also use eye contact to gather information, both about the other person(s) in the communicative interchange and the message involved within the interchange. We often look at another's eyes to try to discern the intent of his message—was he kidding or serious? Is he being open or defensive in his communication? Questions like these are often difficult to answer by examining only the verbal content of the message. Additional factors must be consulted, and eye contact plays an important part. It is not unusual to ascribe certain characteristics to people because of their use of eye contact. For example, former President Nixon was sometimes referred to as "Tricky Dick" because of his habit of having minimal eye contact with his audience. We often believe that people who do not look us straight in the eye are insincere, dishonest, and not worthy of our trust.

Eye contact also is used to monitor and regulate the communication process itself. Throughout any such interchange, be it person-to-person or person-to-group, the intensity of eye contact varies greatly over a period of time. Our attention intensity varies throughout any communicative interchange, and eye contact is used to constantly monitor the progress of the situation. Additionally, eye contact serves as a communication regulator, often controlling what is being said as well as what is about to be said. All of us have experienced the receipt of a "sharp look" that has made us stop short. A teacher often casts a menacing, negative glance towards the class troublemaker, causing him to stop squirming or making noise. Not a word was said by the teacher, but the nonverbal message was loud and clear: "Stop causing a disturbance or you'll be in big trouble!"

This regulatory function also operates in less tense situations as well. A brief, sharp look can communicate the idea that you are unhappy with a speaker's demeanor or message. It can give approval or disapproval, and it can signal the end of the communicative interchange.

A third type of nonverbal communication involves the general movement and posturing of the bodies of the speaker and listeners. You may have seen a speaker who had a great desire to put forth a message, who moved closer to the audience, appeared erect and dynamic, and was quite physically involved in the speech. Such a posture clearly indicates that the speaker has something to say, and this energy and enthusiasm is communicated to the audience. Conversely, the speaker who constantly slouches, who hides behind the podium, and who shies away from the audience conveys a totally different nonverbal message. Such a speaker appears to lack confidence, and it would not be unusual for the audience to expect the worst, not the best, of the speaker.

Similarly, body posture of the audience can be quite meaningful to the speaker during the presentation of a message. An audience slouched in their chairs, squirming about, or looking around the room would indicate that they are bored with the speaker's message. The corresponding nonverbal message would be clear: "Shut up and sit down!" At that point, you should recognize this desire to end communication and restructure your message to regain audience attention and interest. When the audience begins to show signs of restlessness and boredom, enliven your message with a change of message content, a variance in delivery rate, a funny story, or anything that will rekindle the spark of audience interest. Body motions can be of great assistance to the speaker in monitoring the reactions of an audience.

Thus, the physical aspects of nonverbal communication can be visualized as important communicative devices in all situations. Attitudes, reactions, desires, and predispositions are often communicated through the human body. You should use these nonverbal cues to aid in the effective transmission of your message and to better analyze your audience and their reactions to your message.

Verbal Elements

The pitch of the speaker's voice conveys a variety of meanings to an audience. For example, a high, strained voice often indicates that the speaker is under pressure, is concerned or excited about the speech topic or the speaking situation, or is nervous, tense, or afraid. You may well recall your first public speaking experience. In all probability, you were quite nervous, afraid that you were going to make a fool of yourself. However, the "day of reckoning" finally arrived, and as you opened your mouth you were probably surprised at the sound that came out. Instead of having the cool, composed voice that you normally had, you sounded shrill and tense—in fact, you could hardly claim that voice to be your own. Your nervousness carried over into your vocal quality, and everyone in the room knew that you were nervous.

Or suppose that some topic had you very upset and you wanted the audience to become as involved in the topic as you were. This desire to emphasize the topic's importance may have been translated into a heightened pitch quality that indicated the significance of the topic in your own mind. When people become overly emotionally involved with a subject, it is quite normal that their pitch height increases with their in-depth commitment to the subject.

Listeners make judgments based upon the pitch quality of the speaker's voice. The content of the message may be banal and reportorial in construction, but if the pitch is high and strident, the audience will make a judgment based upon the quality of the voice. You should use your vocal pitch to maximize the intent and impact of your message. If your purpose is to coolly inform your audience about something, then your pitch height should be controlled and mellow. If your purpose is to cast "hellfire and damnation" upon some issue, then the pitch height should indicate that message quality. Above all, the pitch height must be consonant with the content and purpose of your message. Any lack of congruence between content and tone of expression will confuse the audience, and the audience will tend to place greater credibility on the tone of the message delivery than on the words themselves.

Similar to the role and importance of vocal pitch, the intensity of the speaker's tone will play a great part in conveying meaning. Vocal intensity deals with the loudness/softness of the speaking voice, but it goes beyond whether or not the speaker can be heard by the audience. Varying the intensity of tone is an effective device in emphasizing important words, terms, or ideas within the speech. Raising or lowering the voice will add emphasis to particular points of a speech, because it sets part of the message aside from the words around it. You should consider using this device to make certain that important points within your speech stand out in the minds of your listeners.

Studies indicate that approximately 65 percent of the meaning we ascribe to a message comes from nonverbal communicative cues. That is, nearly two-thirds of the meanings we attach to messages come, not from the mere verbalization of language, but from the way in which words are uttered and from the physical movements of the speaker. Without any sort of training, all of us become surprisingly expert at both perceiving and interpreting nonverbal cues. As children we come to know what is meant by mother's caressing touch when we are picked up from the crib and cuddled; we know the meaning and importance of no when we are about to knock over a vase or touch a burner on the stove. As we grow, we see other nonverbal stimuli and attach important meanings to them as we come to learn the truth of the saying that it is possible to say one thing but mean another.

Because so much of the meaning ascribed to verbal messages comes from the corresponding nonverbal stimuli, it is critically important that the verbal and nonverbal messages be congruent, that they say the same thing to the audience. What happens, however, when these stimuli do not match, when they are incongruent? In general, when there is a contradiction between verbal and nonverbal cues, the audience will place greater credibility in the nonverbal stimuli and their interpretations of those stimuli. Thus, it is quite possible to have one's message effectively refuted by contradictory nonverbal cues.

Because of the overall importance of nonverbal communication and the specific importance of verbal-nonverbal congruence in the transmission of messages, you must work upon this avenue of expression carefully. Nonverbal expression must be consistent with the intent of your message; there must be congruence between the two. The best written, best organized, and best researched speech can be made ineffective through the use of inappropriate nonverbal signals. Besides asking yourself what your message tells your audience, you must also find out what your physical movements and vocal qualities convey.

Notes

Chapter 2

What Happens When You Communicate

1. See James E. Sayer, *Functional Speech Communication* (Dubuque, Iowa: Kendall/Hunt, 1977), chapter 6.
2. This S-M-C-R analysis is based upon David K. Berlo, *The Process of Communication* (New York: Holt, Rinehart and Winston, 1960).
3. This often is termed the "exigence" for communicating by communication and rhetorical scholars who note that we tend to communicate for rational, as opposed to arbitrary, reasons.
4. This is a truism for semanticists. Writers such as S. I. Hayakawa (now U. S. senator from California), C. K. Ogden, and I. A. Richards promulgated this now-accepted view of language and meaning.
5. Not only has nonverbal communication been a popular area for academic study, it has been popular in general circulation materials. See, for example, Julius Fast, *Body Language* (New York: Pocket Books, 1971).

3

Finding a Subject

"I don't know why they asked me to speak! I really don't know anything. What do they expect me to say?" "What am I going to do? I'm no expert or authority or anything like that. I'll just bore everybody. Why did they pick me to speak? What am I going to say?" If you have little background in public speaking, you have probably uttered remarks similar to these. Why have you been chosen to give a speech? What are you going to speak about? What are you going to do?

One reason for your anxiety about selecting a topic may be your natural tendency to want to do too much. Without admitting it even to yourself, you may wish to present the greatest oratorical pronouncement in the history of mankind. You may wish to put together *the* speech for all generations. You want to offer a speech that would make the great orators of the past green with envy. Besides being unrealistic, such expectations add to your frustration in finding a suitable topic. If you want to set the world on its ear through just one speech, you could spend years searching for the right topic for that presentation.

Instead of setting unrealistic goals for yourself and your speech, you should approach subject selection calmly and rationally. This chapter is designed to acquaint you with a viable

method for finding speech topics. We will begin by examining
the suitability of possible subjects.

PROFILE OF A GOOD SUBJECT

Your chosen subject should be appropriate. *Appropriateness*
is an elusive word, for it has to do with the notion of taste or
suitability. Basically, you want to deal with a subject that is
appropriate to you, to your audience, and to the occasion upon
which you speak. As you consider appropriateness, you will
receive valuable clues to possible topics for your speech.

First, examine yourself—your personality, interests, and favorite activities. This self-examination is critical, for it can
indicate the kinds of subjects that you might enjoy speaking
about. If, for example, you are interested in coin collecting,
spelunking, or pottery, you may find that your hobby fits a
particular audience and speaking occasion. Many service
groups, such as the Kiwanis and Rotary Clubs, devote part of
their get-togethers to informational presentations. Hobby-
related subjects would be quite appropriate under such circumstances. In all situations, the best place to begin your topic
search is between your own ears, for you know far more about
many things than you realize. If you can tap this "hidden
knowledge," then you will be a step up on your search for a
suitable topic.[1]

Second, besides considering your hobbies and other leisure
time interests, think about elements of your job that might be
appropriate and interesting to your audience. Few of us know
the ins and outs of others' occupations, including plumbing,
driving a bus, teaching, taking care of a home, and so on. Many
of these inside bits of information can be quite humorous, and
a funny speech often is appropriate.[2]

Third, have you had any unusual experiences that others
would like to hear about? Have you been through a tornado or
hurricane? Were you ever stranded in a snowstorm? People are
always interested in things that happen to other people.[3] Your
personal experiences do not have to be as cataclysmic as those

real-life dramas you read about in magazines, but they should be generalized enough to let your audience see themselves in the same sort of situation.[4]

Besides examining yourself for potential speech topics, also consider the audience to whom you will speak. Find out all you can about that audience—its purpose for coming together, its interests and activities. Few audiences meet arbitrarily; most groups are formed for a purpose, and an appropriate topic would be one that plugs into that purpose.

Some groups have special interests or pet projects: the support of children's hospitals, providing playground equipment for schoolyards, supporting research in cures for disease, aiding elderly citizens, protecting animals, and so on. A topic that dealt with a group's reason for existence not only would prove to be appropriate subject matter, but it would be a guarantee for rapt audience attention. Therefore, do not face any audience "cold." Find out as much as you can about that audience, and then take advantage of this information by selecting a topic that dovetails with the group's interests.

Finally, an appropriate topic should coincide with the occasion upon which you speak. You may be asked to deliver a Fourth of July speech, and that invitation itself ought to tell you of the preferred subject matter. However, on other less-obvious occasions, check the history books about the day you will speak. Has an important event taken place on that date in the past? Is that day monumental for some reason or another? Is it the anniversary of something of particular significance to that audience?[5]

If you were asked to speak during National Secretaries' Week, a speech dealing with the importance of secretaries would be very appropriate. A speech dealing with political issues would be highly appropriate during the midst of a national political campaign, so long as your analysis was not trite or too simplistic. A sports-oriented topic during the World Series or Super Bowl week would be appropriate, and other such subjects come easily to mind. The advantage of this approach is that your topic takes advantage of the audience's heightened awareness of the topic area. A speech concerning sports medicine would be of great interest during the National Football League's playoff period, because people's awareness of sports would be at a high level.

No matter how you select your topic, one caveat must be held in mind: your topic, and your approach to that topic, must be in good taste; it must not offend or insult your audience.[6] A humorous treatment of the issue of rape would not be in good taste, nor would jokes about abortion and birth control. While the topic of pornography certainly would be of interest to most audiences, the graphic display of pornographic materials clearly would violate any definition of taste and common sense. Perhaps your own common sense is the best barometer of appropriateness, and you should use that measuring device in the selection of your speech topics.

Good topics are interesting. It should go without saying that you ought to choose only topics that will interest your particular audience. Unfortunately, too many speakers apparently forget this rather obvious benchmark of topic suitability. Many speakers assume that anything that interests them must also interest their audiences—a most untenable assumption. Thus, Mark is interested in nuclear waste disposal, so he prepares a speech on that topic without considering the interests of his audience. Sharon likes to spend her leisure time working with macrame, so she speaks for twenty minutes on making various macrame items—to a group of middle-aged businessmen. Walt began collecting baseball cards as a young boy and continued collecting them until well into his twenties. Regardless of the audience or the occasion, Walt always speaks about his baseball card collection.

All three speakers committed the same mistake: they assumed that their own personal interests would be of significance and interest to their audiences. Instead of making this disastrous assumption, you must be certain that your topic will interest your audience as well as yourself. Again, what you can learn about your audience in pre-speech preparation will pay handsome dividends in final speech impact. Information about a group's purpose(s), activities, and future plans will provide very clear indications about that group's interests, and this information, in turn, will help you select a topic for your presentation. For example,

- a humane society would be interested in any topic dealing with animal welfare.
- a consumer group would be interested in new product developments and recent product liability decisions.
- a PTO/PTA group would be interested in any topic pertaining to education—school discipline, financing a college education, and so on.
- a business group would be interested in new government regulations and the cost of such regulations.
- a political action group would be interested in such matters as campaign financing, political ethics, and the "selling" of political candidates.

The potential topics are endless, but the critical point remains the same: the speaker must be concerned with the audience's interests in selecting a topic.

To maximize your topic's interest value, you should demonstrate the usefulness of your topic for your audience; you must show your audience why they need to hear the information you are presenting. Since all of us are bombarded daily with millions of words, it is fairly easy to ignore much of what we hear (consider how many television commercials you see each day but do not really notice). Present your information so that audience interest is attained and maintained throughout your speech. The most effective way to achieve this goal is to prove to your audience that they need to know the material you are presenting.

This need to know is best accomplished by demonstrating your topic's pertinence to the individual audience members. The issue of nuclear waste disposal might appear to be boring, but an intelligent speaker would make that topic vitally interesting by showing the *direct dangers posed to each member of the audience* from nuclear waste. Now the topic is no longer a vague academic concern; now it relates to everyone in the audience, and they will be most interested in the presentation because they can see the topic's relevance to them.

All topics must be shown to be relevant to each audience. The audience must be given a reason to listen to your speech rather than to daydream or take a nap. The best way to gain and hold audience interest is to prove that your speech's content is of direct value, benefit, or consequence to your audience.

Successful topics are limited in scope. Far too many speakers make the mistake of trying to cover a topic too broad for the time allotted. In most speaking situations, you will have an idea as to how many minutes you should speak. To be an effective speaker, you must select a topic that can be handled within the stated time limitations.

I was amused several years ago by a speaker who was given twenty minutes to speak and who decided to select as his topic "Communism: Yesterday, Today, and Tomorrow." Even a casual glance at that topic should indicate that it was too broad for such a short speech. Not surprisingly, the resultant speech was a total disaster. Because the speaker tried to do too much, he virtually flew through his material at a rapid delivery rate, touching but superficially upon a myriad of topics. As a result, the audience came away from that speech totally confused; they had heard many sweeping statements with little or no supporting material to clarify what had been said. Because that speaker selected a topic that simply could not be covered within his time constraints, his speech was predestined to disaster— and the audience was the ultimate loser in this example of dysfunctional communication.

Remember, you cannot cover the entire world in a ten-minute speech. You cannot tell your audience everything about anything in a single presentation. Limit your topic. You cannot cover the entire continent of Africa in one speech, but you can present information about one African tribe. You cannot tell your audience about "1001 Uses for Hamburger," but you can make the same point while limiting your examples to two or three such uses.

Presenting a coverable topic often goes beyond topic choice itself; it often is a matter of proper organization. Most topics, at least at the outset, are too broad to be meaningfully handled in one short oral presentation. The next chapter will deal with the organization of speech materials, presenting you with a specific system that will help you to focus and narrow your topics.

In sum, you ought to remember that those speech topics are best that (1) are appropriate—to you, to the audience, and to the occasion; (2) are interesting—both to you and to your audience; and (3) are coverable—your topic should fit within the time constraints given for your speech. If your speech topic meets those three requirements, then your topic will be of interest and value to your audience, and you will be a more effective speaker.

FINDING A TOPIC

Finding a speech topic is easy—in fact, a good topic probably is inside your head at this moment. As noted earlier in this chapter, the best source for all speech topics lies between your ears, although most people are completely unaware of this gold mine of information. Instead of taking a few minutes to review their own interests and what they already know about a wide variety of topics, many prospective speakers panic: "My God, what am I going to talk about??!!" With this as a first reaction, the rest of the scenario is not going to be pleasant for our all-too-nervous speaker.

After the initial panic, frenzied activity sets in. First, the prospective speaker makes several harried phone calls to close friends, asking their advice about possible topics. Often, this proves unsatisfactory, so the speaker-to-be selects another cure-all: the library. A library is a fine resource for finding

information, but you have to know what you want to find
before you begin scouring the stacks. However, with no idea of
what to talk about, our speaker merely wanders about the
library seeking Divine Intervention in the selection of a speech
topic, hoping that a book will somehow fall open to a suitable
topic area.

All of this is a waste of time. Why should your friends know
more about your potential speech topic than you? What good
is aimless wandering through a library? Moreover, I have it
from the highest authority that God is very busy, too busy to
be concerned about inspiring your forthcoming speech topic.
So, this is one problem you have to face on your own, but it is
a problem that can be faced easily—if you are willing to deal
with the problem in an organized manner.

First, as suggested before, think about your own interests,
activities, and hobbies. How do you spend your time? What
matters interest you? What do you enjoy doing or reading
about? What do you talk about in restful conversations with
your friends? If you will ask yourself those questions, you may
find that the answers will provide several possible topics for
your speech.

Second, what do you know about your audience? What purpose brings this group together? What are this group's goals or
aims? What group projects/activities do you know about?
What other speech topics has this group heard? While you may
not know the answers to those questions, a member of that
group most certainly would, so ask the group's chairman or
president to provide the information you need.[7]

Third, is there anything special about the occasion upon
which you have been asked to speak? Is the day important to
your audience? Does the occasion commemorate a national or
religious holiday? Is it a "special day" in history? Consulting an
almanac or a history book can reveal hidden sources of potential occasion-related topics.

Finally, if your own interests, information about the group,
or speech date significance do not yield viable, suitable topics
for your speech, you can utilize the technique of *brainstorming.*

This technique calls forth, in a random and haphazard manner, all issues that are of conscious value to your mind. Its application is simple:

1. Find a quiet place where you can be alone with pencil and paper.

2. Jot down every thought that comes to your mind—frivolous or significant.

3. Continue thinking and writing until you have drained yourself of every possible thought that comes easily to mind.

Now look at your paper. You will find that you have scribbled many ideas on that sheet of paper, and some of them would be quite viable speech topics. Perhaps you have written thirty ideas, but only four appear to be of true speech material. All you need is one topic for your speech.

By way of example, let's say that one of your words was *economy,* since most Americans are aware that our nation's economy is not in good shape. With that as your key word, take another sheet of paper and jot down every thought you have in relation to the word "economy." You will be surprised to find how much you knew about the economy without realizing it.

You now have quite a few possible speech topics. You could speak about the state of the nation's economy, using several of your specific thoughts as subpoints in your speech, or one of your specific thoughts could serve as a speech topic. Regardless, you now have something with which to work. If you want to go to a library, your research will have some foundation and direction.

Brainstorming is an excellent vehicle for generating many topics in the shortest possible time, and it is a technique that underscores the fact that the best source of topics lies initially within the speaker's own mind.

A SAMPLE SPEECH

So far, we have done a lot of talking about speeches without looking at one. The following speech, "LNG—Handle with Care," is a persuasive speech designed to acquaint the listener with the dangers of liquefied natural gas. As you read this speech, examine its contents carefully. Is this a suitable topic for a speech? For what audiences would it be best suited?

While you might conclude that you could never put together such a fine speech, you are wrong! This speech, like all speeches, began with one idea. However, with work, research, and much re-examination, this simple speech became a most effective persuasive instrument. Your next speech may be of this quality!

LNG—Handle with Care[8]

On October 20, 1944, one of the tanks in Cleveland's liquefied natural gas plant suddenly ruptured, releasing over a million gallons of liquefied natural gas. This liquid overflowed into the streets and sewers, where it reverted to its normal gaseous form and exploded with a tremendous force. The gas then seeped into the basements, where it was ignited by the pilot lights of hot water heaters, and blew the houses apart. Entire families died as they tried to escape the deadly inferno that had once been their neighborhood. Firemen watched helplessly as flames shot up a half-mile into the sky, and temperatures reached three thousand degrees. Eventually, the fire burned itself out, leaving 130 dead, 300 injured, and over 14,-000 homeless.

Recently we've heard a lot about Harrisburg, where the use of nuclear power has been brought into question. Thirty-six years ago, the catastrophe in Cleveland was the Three-Mile Island of the liquefied natural gas industry. In the shock and horror that resulted, the industry was shut down for over twenty years—until spin-offs from the space program made it feasible once again. It's only been in the last year that we've started using LNG to any *real* degree. Today, many people believe LNG has tremendous promise as an energy source. Others believe it has tremendous potential—for destruction. A balance needs to be struck between these two extremes, and in order to reach it, it becomes necessary to examine some basic facts about LNG, some problems with storage, transportation and terrorism, and, finally, some potential solutions to these liabilities.

Natural gas is a plentiful by-product of petroleum. We've long recognized it as an energy source, but not as an *economical* alternative, because it would cost too much to transport from overseas. Then scientists discovered that they could liquify the gas by chilling it to 260 degrees below zero. In its liquid form, it occupies only one six-hundredth of its original volume, so LNG instantly became economically feasible. Tankers are almost a thousand feet long. In order to carry the same amount in a gaseous state, they would have to be more than a hundred *miles* long—which is longer than Long Island!

Natural gas does not pollute and can be easily distributed to consumers. For all of these reasons, the growth of LNG has been phenomonal. In February of 1978, LNG made up only one-tenth of one percent of America's gas consumption. But because of President Carter's strong support of LNG, the December 1978 issue of the *Bulletin of Atomic Scientists* estimated that this figure will be up to 7 percent in the mideighties, and 22 percent by the end of the century. In order to push liquefied natural gas, the Carter Administration has rapidly approved numerous sites and facilities, and abolished all import restrictions.

In order to visualize these facts about LNG, I want each of you to imagine a football stadium filled to a depth of 125 feet with liquid gas. That is how much gas is carried by one tanker. Now let's imagine it's warmed back to its gaseous state. Imagine 600 football stadiums filled to that same depth. Now, imagine a lighted match.

It is that nightmarish image that has led some scientists to question the safety of LNG, citing problems with storage, transportation and terrorism. If spilled from a storage tank, LNG will boil rapidly. It will either ignite at the source, or vaporize into a gaseous cloud that will then float downwind. Eventually it will be ignited by anything from a cigarette to an electric spark. The result will make Hiroshima pale by comparison. The May 22, 1977, issue of the *Houston Post* predicts that an LNG spill in New York City would cause more than 800,000 casualties. After the initial explosion, a chain reaction would take effect, with hundreds of petrochemical plants and storage facilities exploding and adding to the holocaust.

The problems with transportation are even worse. Each tanker is a giant thermos bottle, equal to a million tons of TNT —eighty times more powerful than the bomb we dropped on Hiroshima. And all these floating bombs need to be "set off" is contact with air or water. The tank that ruptured in Cleveland had 6200 cubic meters of LNG; tankers today commonly carry 160,000. Captain Richard Simonds of the U.S. Coast Guard said in 1978, "We've just been plain lucky so far. A major LNG incident must occur. We are just waiting. It's a question of when, not if." Furthermore, transportation problems are not limited just to ships. Oversized trucks on our highways and tankcars on our railroads are being used as well. So now this nightmare extends to include rush-hour traffic.

In addition to problems with storage and transportation, LNG proponents have to cope with the growing spectre of terrorism. Drs. Andrew Van Horn and Richard Wilson, of the Energy and Environmental Policy Center, admit that "the threat of sabotage may well represent the largest risk to the public from LNG facilities." Wilson noted that he himself had been able to get close enough to the valves of a storage tank to let the gas escape, without being challenged.

With the rate terrorism has been growing over the last five years, we cannot ignore this problem. It doesn't take much imagination to picture the political ramifications if an American LNG tanker should be sabotaged and cause a holocaust in a foreign port—whether friendly or hostile.

Obviously, what we are facing here is a very frightening dilemma. We would be foolish to ignore the fact that LNG is a clean, cheap and innovative answer to the energy crisis. But we would be irresponsible to ignore the threat to the public safety. In trying to find an answer to this dilemma, we have to come to terms with two very harsh facts. First, no matter what energy source we choose, there is going to be an element of risk, and, sadly, an element of loss. The key to using LNG is to minimize the risk as much as possible. The second harsh reality is that whether or not we support the decision, America is going to use liquefied natural gas. Our short-term energy needs outweighed the long-term safety problems, so the tankers are in our harbors right now. The point is, since we have to use LNG, let's use it wisely and safely.

The dangers of storage could be greatly lessened by more government controls. As Representative Edward Markey said two years ago, "At the LNG safety hearing, witness after witness testified as to the failure of the federal government to provide a coordinated LNG policy to protect the public health and safety." Right now, a dozen different agencies claim jurisdiction over LNG. One comprehensive department might eliminate the fiascoes, such as the proposed storage site right under the approach of a California airport's runway. They could also implement frequent and thorough inspections and push international controls. We've all heard the jokes about bureaucracy, where one hand doesn't know what the other is doing, but it is important to remember that in this case, one hand is literally playing with fire. LNG is simply too dangerous to be allowed to exist without more stringent controls.

The dangers of transportation could be eased, first of all, by either eliminating or restricting the use of highways and railroads to transport LNG. We could also greatly reduce the number of possible victims. Experts have never been able to understand why we installed LNG terminals in highly populated areas like New York, Atlanta and Los Angeles. They say LNG ports should only be allowed on relatively unoccupied coastlines. Recently, California (which is about to become a major LNG market) made remote siting mandatory for LNG facilities. So it *can* be done. While this sensible switch is taking place, America could develop offshore terminals, using both natural islands and man-made floating harbors.

Terrorism is always difficult to control, but once we've

removed these terminals from highly populated areas, we've removed much of the terrorist's motivation. The threat of sabotage isn't nearly as frightening when these floating bombs aren't in New York's harbor, or floating up the Mississippi River. In addition to this, the lax security restrictions need to be much more stringent. The National Task Force on Disorders and Terrorism backs up both these proposals, concluding that if the number of potential victims is kept small and the facility is well protected, the act of terrorism is no longer considered worthwhile.

If these solutions are put into effect, the problems with storage, transportation and terrorism are greatly lessened, and LNG becomes an acceptable, and even welcome, servant. But if the situation is allowed to escalate under the present conditions, LNG could well trigger a disaster that mankind would never be able to forget or forgive. Just as nuclear power proponents will have to cope with the memory of Harrisburg, so should those who urge the rebirth of LNG remember the disaster in Cleveland that caused it to die in the first place. The whole issue of liquefied natural gas can be summed up in one simple comparison. The cargo of one tanker can provide a year's supply of energy for a city of 30,000 Americans. It also provides the capability to burn down that same city. Let's not forget *either* fact.

Notes

Chapter 3

Finding a Subject

1. All of us subconsciously remember a great deal of information, much more than we consciously realize. We need to tap this area of hidden knowledge, principally through the process of brainstorming explained at the end of this chapter.

2. A most interesting public speaking form is the after-dinner speech, a speech that presents serious, informative material in a humorous and/or satirical manner.

3. All of us are vitally interested in items that affect other people. The popularity of *People* magazine and such television shows as "Real People" and "That's Incredible" underscore this fact.

4. Some years ago, Kenneth Burke coined the term *identification* to indicate this speaker-audience factor: "You persuade a man only insofar as you can talk his language by speech, gesture, tonality, order, image, attitude, idea, identifying your ways with his."

5. Many newspapers have a column entitled "This Date in History," a quick reference source for history-related speech topics.

6. Hugh Blair, in "Lectures on Rhetoric and Belles Lettres," published many times during the 1700s, noted that the effective communicator needed to cultivate "critical judgment," an essential element of good taste.

7. Since the group's chairman or president certainly wants your

speech to be a success, this person will be happy to provide you with whatever information you require to make your speech successful.

8. "LNG—Handle with Care," by Suzanne Lindsey, delivered at the National Forensic Association's national speech tournament in Whitewater, Wisconsin, on April 16, 1979. Used with the permission of Miss Lindsey.

4

Organizing Your Thoughts

"I'm not really sure what she said. I think she had some fine ideas, but, truthfully, I kept getting lost. What do *you* think she said?" All of us have felt or said something like this at least once in our lives. We have been confused by the disorganized ramblings of a speaker—a politician, preacher, teacher, or the guest speaker at a meeting. Whatever the surroundings, the effect of a disorganized speech is the same: a dismayed, confused, and frustrated audience, the guaranteed makings for miscommunication.

Effective public speaking demands that a speaker exhibit a logical structure of presentation and that the contents of a speech be functionally organized for maximum audience comprehension and agreement. In short, your finest speech topic, supported by outstanding research information, will be worthless if your material is not organized effectively. Many people will not be able to understand your message if it is disorganized; they will become a "non-audience" because of your helter-skelter pattern of topic presentation.[1]

On the other hand, some people can make sense of disorganized material, but they will be affronted at having to mentally re-organize your speech, and your credibility (and persuasiveness) as a speaker will suffer.[2] Perhaps you have listened to a disorganized speech, but through intense effort you were able to make sense of what was said. How did you feel about the speaker who put you through such torture? Maybe you said something like this: "What a jerk! His ideas were okay, but I had to figure them out for myself! I resent having to do the speaker's job for him!" That is not an uncommon reaction, and it is one that you certainly do not want to instill in your audience.

Many years ago, the ancient Roman rhetoricians taught their students a five-step method for effective speaking: (1) the invention or discovery of ideas; (2) organization of materials; (3) style —the use of language; (4) effective delivery of the speech; and (5) memory—the memorization of speeches and speech materials.[3] As you can see, the classical teachers of rhetoric knew how important organization was for effective public speaking. Effective organization is just as important today—perhaps more so, because there are many more distractions that can cause an audience's attention to wander. Today's speakers have to contend with noise and audience movement. All of us are competing indirectly with the entertainment medium of television. Organization is important, and effective organization is the result of a planned, methodical approach to speech construction. This chapter is designed to acquaint you with the basics of effective speech organization.

GATHERING INFORMATION

Many speakers get into trouble right away by failing to realize that the organization of speech materials should *follow* the accumulation of needed research information. If you think about it for a moment, you will realize that organization can take place only after the content ideas and information for the speech have been found. However, too many speakers try to put the cart before the horse.

Alicia was asked to speak to a local neighborhood group about "Today's Problem of Inflation." Agreeing to present such a speech, she immediately sat down and outlined the ideas she wanted to speak about. Then, with outline in hand, she went to her local library to find the material needed to support her ideas. Much to her dismay, Alicia found that many of the materials she needed did not exist (at least her local library did not have them), so she had to revise her speech to include only those materials she was able to find.

As you can see, Alicia wasted a great deal of time and thought in trying to organize her speech before being absolutely certain that she could find the necessary support materials for her speech. Instead of proceeding logically, Alicia organized her speech before going to the library, only to find that many needed materials could not be secured. The result: Alicia had to go back to square one, revising the entire preplanned speech to include only those matters for which she was able to find supporting information. In short, she had to organize her speech twice, wasting valuable planning and research time in the process.

You cannot organize something before you know what that something is. Since most of us are too busy to afford wasting time, we ought to make the most of our pre-speech preparations. Follow three steps for efficient preparation:

1. After developing (speaker-created) or receiving (imposed by another, as in Alicia's "Today's Problem of Inflation") your speech topic, take several minutes to jot down what you know about the topic area. (This is the brainstorming process.)

2. Take your list of potential speech contents to the library; use it as your guide for locating specific supporting information.

3. After completing your research, organize your speech, placing your ideas and their supporting materials in a logical pattern.

Organization comes *after* your research efforts have been completed, allowing you to know what you can say (and support) and what you cannot. This sequence helps you use your time effectively; you will not have to return to square one, because each step is based upon information secured in each preceding step.

RESEARCH MATERIALS

Many beginning public speakers are frightened by the prospect of having to do research—of having to invade the dank, musty reaches of a library. As with the fear of public speaking itself, this concern about research springs primarily from the speaker's mind, creating a negative mental image of hours of unenjoyable drudgery.

Research does not have to be like that, as long as you are willing to conduct your research methodically. Unfortunately, too many people have no method for their research activities, and these people suffer. You can easily spot them in any library: they wander about aimlessly, eyes glazed, with a perpetual scowl of worry. To avoid such a plight, you must approach your research task realistically and with positive expectations. Overall, you merely want to find some basic information that will support or prove the main points of your speech. You are *not* trying to glean information to help you earn the Nobel Prize in physics. You need not be concerned with the technical vagaries of research applicable to scholarly articles or doctoral dissertations; you need to secure basic information for preparing your speech.

With that research perspective in mind, you may begin your library work, moving from generalized to more specific research activities. First, you should have a list of possible subjects to research (those ideas generated via the brainstorming process discussed in chapter 3) with you when you go to the library. At this point, you want to secure general research information that will help you determine which ideas to include within your final speech. The best place to start your research is with the card catalog.

Every library, regardless of size or holdings, has a card catalog which serves as the virtual cornerstone of the library's reference area. Since the catalog contains a listing for every book held by the library, this source will divulge many useful "leads" for your research.[4] Filed within the catalog in alphabetical order are three types of cards: subject cards, author cards, and title cards. You will find the subject cards to be most useful in starting your research. Subject cards headed with your topic ("Inflation") will tell you the titles of books on your topic, their authors and dates of publication, and the specific subjects covered within each book. This information allows you to decide if a book will be of value to you before you try to locate it on the shelves.

A second source of general research information is the library's collection of periodicals—various news magazines and journals. Periodicals are the most up-to-date sources of information you can secure. The *Reader's Guide to Periodical Literature* is the best known and most prevalent source for periodicals listings, especially for items of general subjects or current events. As with the subject cards in the card catalog, each volume of the *Reader's Guide* is organized alphabetically by subject. Each reference contains the title of a pertinent article, its author, and the name, volume, and page numbers of the periodical in which the article may be found. *The Reader's Guide* will help you find material in popular magazines such as *Time, Newsweek,* and other widely circulated periodicals.

As you look through the books and articles on your topic, you will come across a lot of information, too much to memorize. You ought to take notes about what you read, perhaps recording verbatim items of particularly important information. You should have a coherent note-taking system, not try to jot down materials on scraps of paper. I have found that putting information on note cards is the best way to organize research materials, placing one piece of information on a separate card. When you have completed your library research, you will have a series of note cards to rearrange and consult as you plan the major content of your speech.[5] (See Figure 4.1).

At this point, you might wonder exactly what to look for as you conduct your research. Basically, the information you want

Author
Title
Source
Publication Date

"Since laboratory studies often do not relate to the real world, researchers must concentrate more upon applied field experiments."

Fig. 4.1 Recording research information on a note card.

to secure will present ideas and supporting material on your topic area. If your speech topic were "Today's Problem of Inflation," you would want to find materials that define the problem, exemplify the problem, and indicate possible causes and solutions. In short, you want to find specific materials that make the topic of inflation as clear to your audience as possible; you want to do more than speak in banal generalities.

Regardless of your topic, your research should center upon the acquisition of two types of materials: factual information and opinionated information. These materials will help you to concretize and illustrate the major ideas within your speech. Factual information consists of two types of material—real-life examples and statistical data—which may easily be found within most books and periodicals.

The following real-life example might be secured from library research. Mary Doherty went to the grocery store last week to buy a gallon of milk. She paid $2.17. Two years ago, that same gallon of milk would have cost $1.39. On her way home, she stopped for a quick lunch and paid $2.00 for a Big Mac, a small order of fries, and a small Coke. Ten years ago, that same meal would have cost $.81. Mary's experience shows the real meaning of inflation.

Such examples are effective, because they clearly illustrate a point being made by a speaker. Instead of speaking about the impact of inflation in vague, general terms, the example of Mary Doherty "brings home" that impact in terms with which the speaker's audience can identify. All of us have experienced the same price trauma as Mary; we can see the same things happening to us. Since all of us are interested in matters that affect other people, the use of real-life examples is an excellent way to simultaneously illustrate a point and retain audience interest and attention.

A second type of factual information is statistical data. We use statistics all the time—in fact, the preceding example of Mary Doherty contained several bits of statistical information (the specific cost of a gallon of milk and Mary's lunch). Books and magazine articles contain many sets of statistical data: percentages (8 percent of the nation's labor force is unemployed), ratios (four out of five doctors recommend jogging for weight control), and raw statistical data (it is estimated that over 100,000 illegal aliens reside within the United States). Such helps to make a point clear and specific. Certainly, as an audience member, you learn more about a situation when it is specified statistically than when it is generalized. You learn more by hearing that "8 percent of the labor force is unemployed" than by hearing that "quite a lot of people are out of work."

One word of caution ought to be issued concerning the use of statistical data. Since few people are familiar with the way that statistics are generated and how such information can be interpreted and misinterpreted, many members of your audience may be misled or confused by this type of information.[6] Therefore, you must be careful to explain clearly the nature and meaning of your statistical data, and you must never include so many statistics that your audience gets lost in a confusing sea of numbers. Some speakers mistakenly assume that statistics speak for themselves. The statistic "38 percent" does not mean a thing until I put meaning to it by explaining that the number refers to something ("Thirty-eight percent of all high school students complete a college degree within six years after high school graduation"). Each bit of statistical data must be explained; otherwise, your audience will become confused, and the rationale for using statistics—clarity—will be lost.

In addition to factual material, you may want to use some opinionated material: statements from subject-matter experts that support your point of view or better illustrate the issue you intend to speak about. Most books and magazine articles are written to make a point, often to advocate a political, social, or economic position on the part of the writer. Your reading is full of opinionated information like this statement by Massachusetts Lieutenant Governor O'Neill at the Hearings on Railroad Revitalization. "Railroads are four times more energy efficient than are trucks, and sixty times more efficient than air-craft. At the same time they contribute less pollution than does any other form of transportation."

Such opinionated information provides information *per se* and also buttresses your contention that we ought to use our railroads more to combat our ever-worsening energy crisis. Your position is strengthened by the support of another person, thereby making your point or contention more credible and more persuasive.

As with statistical data, you must be careful in the use of opinionated information. Simply being published in a book or magazine does not make a statement accurate—or even true. Since most writers have an axe to grind when they write their books or essays, it is not uncommon for exaggerations or com-plete misstatements to occur. You should take opinionated information with the proverbial grain of salt and try to make sure that your "expert" is correct. At a minimum, you want to know that your source of information has the right to make the statement you intend to quote. As a receiver of information, you should not accept the analyses and judgments of so-called experts until you are satisfied that these people have the posi-tion, training, and experience to offer such information.

All too often speeches are full of questionable citations such as this: "A highly placed unnamed White House official says that the president does not intend to impose any kind of wage and price controls to offset the continuing spiral of inflation." While that information might appear to be compelling at first glance, careful scrutiny shows that you should not have great faith in the content of that citation. Who is this "unnamed White House official?" Are you willing to accept the statement of an unnamed source? After all, the third-floor janitor at the White House would, by definition, qualify as being "highly placed." You should avoid using such source citations, and you certainly ought to be very hesitant about accepting the claims and conclusions offered by such unspecified sources.

Research information, then, serves to illustrate and substantiate the internal contents of your speech. You will have to do some external digging in putting together most of your oral presentations. You will discover that the actual accumulation of basic research information is a relatively easy task, one that requires your usage of easily found references within your local library.

TYPES OF ORGANIZATION

Once you have secured the necessary research materials for your speech, your next concern is initial development of the general structure of your speech. Your goal is to package your material in such a way that it will be understood and accepted by your audience. In fact, you ought to see your organizational efforts as the development of a master strategy—a plan for presenting material with maximum effectiveness.

You may choose from four major types of organizational strategies: chronological, spatial, process or example, and topical.

The Chronological Pattern

Some subjects must be developed within a particular time frame. For example, were I to speak about "The Development of the Military Draft in the United States," I might approach my topic chronologically by following this pattern:

    I. Introduction: The Draft in American History
    II. Body: Charting the Development of the Draft
        A. Conscription During the Civil War
        B. The Draft and World War One
        C. The Draft and World War Two
        D. The "Peacetime" Draft: Korea and Vietnam
        E. The Volunteer Army of the 1970s
    III. Conclusion: Future Prospects of the Draft

As you can see, the central speech organization would be based upon the development of the speech topic over the passage of time—how the military draft was started, when it was

used, and changes that have been made. The chronological
pattern allows the audience to see how your topic has developed
over whatever time period you decide to select.

The Spatial Pattern

Although this organizational structure is used infrequently
by speakers, you should be aware of its existence in case you
happen to find it to be useful in the future. Basically, the spatial
pattern is concerned with the relationship of objects in space.
If you were to explain the physical layout of a house, you might
describe the location of the living room in relation to the
kitchen, the bedrooms to the bathrooms, and so on. A television
weather reporter often plots the movement of a storm across a
large land mass, from the Southwest to the Midwest and then
on to the Northeast, exhibiting a spatial study of the storm's
movement. While you probably will not use this organizational
pattern for an entire speech, it might be used for part of a
speech that is concerned largely with physical relationships.

The Process or Example Pattern

Some speeches require that you tell your audience "how to
do it"—how to make a macrame object, how to check the
timing on the family car, or how to put a battery in a watch.
Other speeches require that an extended example be provided
to assure maximum clarity of understanding: the steps to follow
in opening a savings account or perhaps the procedures for
buying stock at a stock exchange. In all such instances, you try
to show your audience how something can or should be done
by providing them with a step-by-step approach to your topic.
These steps essentially form the major components of your
internal organization.

For example, in a speech entitled "How to Diaper a Baby"
the following organizational pattern might be employed:

    I. Introduction
   II. Body: How The Baby Should Be Diapered

    A. Bathing and Powdering the Baby
    B. Folding the Diaper
    C. Placing the Baby on the Diaper
    D. Pinning the Diaper Properly
  III. Conclusion

Often accompanied by visual aids (a baby doll plus diaper would do quite nicely in the preceding example), the speaker is able to take the audience through the process or example slowly and accurately, thereby assuring maximum comprehension of the message. As you would imagine, most training manuals and sets of instructions are organized according to this pattern.

The Topical Pattern

The most used organizational pattern is the topical pattern, one in which the main points are organized in a logical order. In this pattern, the speaker employs the "golden rule" of organization: materials should be presented in such a way that most members of the audience will be able to understand the content of the message. Most speeches do not have a natural chronological, spatial, or process structure; instead, they are an amalgam of materials which must be organized in a logical order. Remember that logical order must be defined in the audience's terms, not the speaker's. That is, the nature of the audience must determine the logic of the organization.

Reread Sue Lindsey's speech, "LNG—Handle with Care," that was presented in chapter 3. You should note that it is organized topically—a logical presentation designed to get you to agree with her point of view. All the items within that speech were carefully arranged by Ms. Lindsey to come together for maximum effectiveness, to secure your agreement that the present use of and future plans for liquefied natural gas are dangerous and ought to be stopped. She considered her audience and how people are often motivated, and the resultant topical pattern led to a powerful and persuasive speech.

Most essays in newspapers and magazines are structured

topically, so you ought to study such examples of public communication to see how topical patterns work. Many of these articles can be revamped into effective oral presentations, for persuasive writers are confronted with most of the same problems that affect speakers. You may learn a great deal about organization by reading the columns of William Buckley, James Reston, and other nationally syndicated writers.

THE SPEECH

Regardless of the particular organization pattern selected, your speech should be divided into three major parts: the introduction (designed to secure audience attention and preview your topic), the body (designed to present the major points of your speech), and the conclusion (designed to summarize the major points made within your speech). Each of these parts will be considered below.[7]

The Introduction

The introduction serves as the starting point of your speech. Because this part of your speech will be the first thing your audience hears from you, you should plan the contents of your introduction carefully. This part of your speech serves two purposes: (1) to gain the attention of your audience and (2) to preview the contents of the body of your speech.

In most speaking situations, gaining your audience's attention is relatively easy, because you will be the only person on the floor. Since most of us have been raised to exhibit politeness to a speaker, when you first take the floor to speak, people tend to be quiet and to give you their attention. (In those rare instances when audience members are not so polite, other members tend to quiet the unruly ones by making loud "shhh" sounds.) However, you should not trust to audience politeness to guarantee their attention. Instead, your introduction should contain an "attention arrestor" that will grab the audience's attention, making them want to hear what you have to say.

There are four major attention arrestors that you may employ:

1. Telling a story or humorous anecdote is a device that has been used by speakers for many years, and this technique works more often than not. Stories and jokes tend to put audiences in a relaxed frame of mind, making them more receptive to your message. However—and this is most important—your story or joke must be pertinent to the subject of your speech. The introduction of a speech is not supposed to be your chance to gag an audience with a series of one-liners or to emulate Henny Youngman. Such non-pertinent introductions do nothing more than lead an audience astray, and many people become upset by hearing irrelevant material.

One final thought about telling jokes: knowing a joke and telling it well are two separate things. Proper delivery, timing, and taste are important in making a funny story truly funny. Therefore, before launching your speech with a joke that you "know will have them on the floor," try it out on several friends to see if it really is funny. Nothing is so devastating to a speaker as an introductory joke that bombs. When your "world's greatest joke" is met with cold stares from your audience, you have put your image in a hole right at the beginning, and the rest of the speech will be an uphill battle. So, before you use a joke, give it a few trial runs.

2. Using startling facts or examples is another effective way of securing audience attention, and it is one that is used a great deal by newscasters at the start of their telecasts ("Ten thousand people are starving in Africa. We'll be back with the news in just a moment."). A fact or example that pertains directly to your specific audience will garner attention. Perhaps this point is best exemplified by the speaker who began his speech about the dangers of cancer by saying, "Six of you in this room will die of cancer within the next five years. You could be one of them." While this is an excellent attention-getting technique, don't force the matter by using some bizarre material that is, at best, only marginally pertinent to your speech. Like a joke

or story, your startling fact or example must be centrally related to the main content of your presentation.

3. Opening your speech with an appropriate quotation from another person generally will secure audience attention, and it is an excellent way to preview the subject of your speech as well. Some speakers use bits of poetry for introductions, or quotations from novels or newspaper stories—almost every possible source of quotable material. Since many speakers find that the most difficult part of any speech is trying to find a good first sentence, the use of quotations provides an easy method for starting the communication process. A book of quotations will come in handy if you decide to open your speech via this method.[8]

4. Finally, using a visual aid will get your audience's attention. Beginning your speech with a picture, chart, slides, or a model of something will grab your audience and make them receptive to your message. Since the proper use of visual aids can be tricky, you should be sure to read the section concerning visual aids in chapter 6.

In addition to the different ways that you can select to open your speech, there are two kinds of introductions you should *not* use in any situation. The first ineffective introduction is used by many speakers: "Tonight I'm going to talk to you about . . ." Not only does that introduction show no creativity on the part of the speaker, it also lets the cat out of the bag much too early. If your audience is not too wild about hearing a speech on your topic, hitting them in the face with it right away will cause many of your audience members to turn you off immediately and not to hear another word that you say. An imaginative introduction sneaks the topic on the audience, thereby increasing your chances of receiving a fair hearing.

The second ineffective type of introduction is one that poses a question to your audience: "Have you ever dabbled in the art of macrame? Tonight I'm going to show you how easy and enjoyable it is." The problem with that introduction is that it assumes that no one will answer the question out loud—a most dangerous assumption. Unfortunately, this scenario can take place:

SPEAKER: Have you ever dabbled in the art of macrame?
AUDIENCE MEMBER: No, and I don't give a damn about it!
SPEAKER: (Silence—while trying to recover from coronary arrest.)

The introductory rhetorical question assumes that no one will actually answer that question, but it takes only one person in your audience to make a shambles of your plans. Instead of starting with a question, it is far better (and safer) to turn that question into a declarative sentence and start from there.

Regardless of the type of introduction used, you need to be absolutely certain about what you are going to say. Since the introduction leads your audience into the body of your speech, it should be a well-prepared and polished speech component. Never leave your introduction to on-the-floor inspiration; never trust that you'll think of an introduction when it's time to begin your speech. Instead, your introduction should be ready for delivery long before your time to speak arrives. The introduction should take only about 5 percent of your speaking time; for example, a twenty-minute speech should have an introduction about one minute long. There is no reason why this speech component should not be memorized almost word for word, and such a well-prepared beginning will help you overcome the stage fright all speakers experience at the opening of a speech.

The Body

The majority of your speaking time will be spent in the delivery of the main portion, or body, of your speech. About 85 percent of your time should be given to the presentation of this part of your speech—or seventeen minutes of a twenty-minute speech.

It is here that you are most concerned about the organization of your material and the pattern that the organization will follow (chronological; spatial; process or example; topical). Remember, however, that the important item in structuring your speech is the logical development of your material for your audience. It is imperative that your information be presented so that your audience will understand your message. You must make certain that, at a minimum, your message is clearly presented.

In putting together your speech, you should outline its contents, just as you were taught to outline essays and term papers in English composition classes in high school. By writing down the main points you wish to emphasize, you can see how your speech looks on paper, and then you can rearrange the outline's points to make more logical sense or to put the material in a more effective sequence. If you write an outline (much as those two hypothetical speeches on the draft and diapering a baby were outlined earlier within this chapter), you will find that organization of your speech will be accomplished more effectively.

The Conclusion

The final part of your speech, the conclusion, is designed to wrap up your presentation neatly and logically. But far too many speakers fail to plan their conclusions, hoping that they will stumble naturally upon an appropriate conclusion while they speak. Such speakers ramble aimlessly, repeat themselves several times, or, once they realize they have nothing left to say, look sheepishly at the audience and say, "Well, that's it. I'm done."

They certainly are. Such an ill-defined and unprepared conclusion leaves a bad taste in the audience's mouth and a feeling of incompleteness about the speech. Since the conclusion is the last part of your speech your audience will hear, you want to leave with a positive, forceful impression, and a "Gee whiz, I guess I'm finished" ending doesn't do the job.

Perhaps the best way to conclude a speech is to summarize the main points you want your audience to remember. Theoretically, a conclusion should be constructed so that someone hearing only that portion of your speech would be able to figure out the thesis of your entire presentation, and a summary of your main points will meet that goal.

As with the introduction, you cannot trust to spur-of-the-moment inspiration for the development of an effective conclusion. It, too, should be planned in advance, consuming 10 percent of your speaking time—two minutes of a twenty-minute speech. Your conclusion should be as well prepared as your introduction, guaranteeing that you will end positively and effectively, creating a favorable final impression with your audience.

THE ORGANIZING PROCESS

To conclude this chapter, let's recap the steps involved in the effective organization of a speech:

1. Select a topic.

2. Conduct preliminary research—both within yourself and by consulting external sources.

3. Conduct more specific research, accumulating the necessary information for your speech.

4. Develop a rough outline of the overall speech.

5. Revise the outline, preparing the introduction and conclusion in detail.

6. Develop the outline of the body of the speech.

7. Revise the outline of the body.

8. Check the structure of the entire speech, making final revisions and adjustments where appropriate.

If you will take the time to follow those eight steps in the organization of your speeches, you will find that their impact will be heightened. You cannot be hurt by being too concerned about speech organization, but your speech can be a disaster if you are not concerned enough. If it is true as Alexander Pope wrote that "Order is Heaven's first law," then it is equally true that "Organization must be the Public Speaker's first responsibility."

Notes

Chapter 4

Organizing Your Thoughts

1. Since most audiences are heterogeneous, composed of many people of differing levels of intelligence, the speaker must be aware of the fact that listeners with a lower level of intelligence simply will not be able to figure out what is intended in a disorganized presentation.

2. Those listeners of high intelligence will be able to understand a disorganized message, but the disorganized speaker will suffer in the eyes of the audience, and the impact of the speech will be severely damaged.

3. Known as "The Five Roman Canons," this pattern of speech study was used by such famous historical and rhetorical figures as Caesar, Cicero, and Quintilian.

4. See *Using the Card Catalog* (Syracuse, N. Y.: New Readers Press, 1971).

5. You will have most success by using the legal-sized notecard that measures four inches by six inches. The recipe card (three inches by five inches) is a bit too small, requiring too many notecards to keep straight.

6. There is a great deal of truth in Prime Minister Benjamin Disraeli's complaint that "There are lies, damn lies, and statistics."

7. The ancient rhetoricians taught students to organize a speech into six parts; today we have consensually agreed to compress those six elements into the three-part structure of introduction, body, and conclusion.

8. These sources organize little bits of quotable material by topic, making them convenient sources for such information.

5

Selling Yourself

For many centuries, teachers of the art of public speaking have written and lectured about the "three modes of proof" originally isolated by teachers of rhetoric in Ancient Greece.[1] Explained simply, these three items were the main factors that made a speech believable to an audience: *logos,* or logically based argument, *pathos,* or emotionally based argument, and *ethos,* or the persuasiveness evinced by the character of the speaker. While all three factors have been found to be significant in causing a speaker's message to be accepted by an audience, no less an authority than Aristotle noted several centuries before the birth of Christ that *ethos* might be the most potent persuasive tool at the disposal of the speaker.

Today we continue to teach the tripartite division of the modes of proof, but we know a great deal more about how these factors work and interrelate in the communication process. *Ethos,* though we tend to refer to this factor as "credibility" or the "speaker's image," is, as Aristotle suggested, significant in helping speakers to achieve their goals. This chapter is designed to acquaint you with the notion of the speaker's image and those factors that will help you to create the kind of image necessary for effective public speaking.

THE SPEAKER'S IMAGE

You do not have to be a communications expert to realize how important image is to the successful public speaker. All of us know people in whom we place a great deal of faith and confidence. We trust these people, whom we call friends, and we tend to respect their word. To us, our friends have a highly positive image; they are credible in our eyes. Conversely, we know other people whom we do not trust much; we tend to question the veracity of what they say. They do not have a positive image, nor do they have much credibility in our view. We do not refer to these people as friends; at best, we might call them "acquaintances."

You will probably find that you respond to and communicate with these differing groups of people in significantly different manners. With your friends, you act and speak respectfully; you treat them as equals in your daily affairs. On the other hand, you are not nearly as respectful to your acquaintances, and you may not be as careful of their feelings. In short, your images of certain people greatly affect your communication with them, including (1) how often you communicate with them, (2) under what circumstances you will communicate with them and (3) the nature and substance of your communication. The more positive the image, the more you will communicate with a person and the more positive the nature of that communication will be.

These interpersonal images come into play in public speaking situations as well as individual encounters. While your message certainly has a great impact upon your audience (the content of your message, how you use language, your style of delivery, and the method of organization), you should realize that who you are and what you are (or how you are perceived to be) have significant impact upon how your audience will react to your message. That is why major political figures spend money during their campaigns to create and maintain a positive image of themselves for the voters. Politicians know that a negative image will be disastrous for them at the polls, so it pays for them to cultivate appropriate images.[2]

When we speak of *ethos,* credibility, or the speaker's image, we deal with a very vague and hard to define concept. Much like the concepts of "charisma" and "morale," the speaker's credibility is a difficult term to pin down. Over the years, the following descriptors have been employed to define the notion of "the speaker's image": truthfulness, honesty, sincerity, virtue, sagacity, benevolence, charity, modesty, intelligence, and wisdom. This listing of descriptors could go on and on, attesting to the complexity of what we call the speaker's image.

One major result of contemporary empirical research has been the delimitation of those factors that appear to be of greatest importance in creating a person's image. Such research has concluded that a person's image is an amalgam of three primary factors: trustworthiness, competence, and dynamism. Each factor will be discussed below.[3]

Trustworthiness

For a positive image, you must show your audience that you are trustworthy, that you are not trying "to pull a fast one" over on them or trying to con them into something that might not be beneficial. It is difficult to believe a speaker who seems untrustworthy. How can you accept the speaker's message if you cannot trust the source of that message?

Two recent political figures have been hampered by questions concerning their trustworthiness. Former President Richard Nixon was often referred to by his detractors as "Tricky Dick," and the Watergate fiasco only solidified this negative image. Senator Edward (Ted) Kennedy of Massachusetts has found that the tragic accident at Chappaquiddick has left lingering doubts about his trustworthiness, and this negative image devastated his campaign for president during the 1980 primaries. While we might recognize and appreciate a person's skills or expertise, we cannot and will not support that individual for high public office if we also believe that person does not merit our trust.

Competence

Your image is directly affected by how your audience assesses your competence in dealing with the topic of your presentation. Do you really know what you are talking about, or are you trying to "bull" your way through your speech? A speaker who is seen as incompetent or unknowledgeable will not be regarded positively, and the speaker's message simply will not be accepted.

Concerns about competence hampered President Jimmy Carter's re-election bid during 1980, because many voters felt that he did not possess the skills necessary to fulfill his White House duties. As Mr. Carter discovered, it is very difficult to have your ideas accepted if your audience believes that you are not competent to generate sound ideas or to implement them.

Dynamism

The final major factor related to image is dynamism, or how a speaker presents a message. In general, audiences prefer to listen to speakers who are outgoing, entertaining, and interesting.

The factor of dynamism appears to be the weakest of the three factors that create the speaker's image. Positive ratings in both trustworthiness and competence tend to offset a negative rating in dynamism, so it seems that you should strive to be seen as trustworthy and competent, with dynamism virtually the icing on the cake. However (and this will be discussed in chapter 6), it is important that you gain and retain audience attention and interest throughout a speech, and the factor of dynamism is particularly important in developing a positive delivery style.

Two additional points about the speaker's image ought to be considered before concluding this section. First, the *initial impact* of the speaker's image on the message of the speech appears to wane with the passage of time. At first, a highly positive impression will carry a significant impact in terms of the acceptance and believability of a speaker's message. However, the speaker's image rating may decline as people begin to re-examine exactly what was said. Conversely, the image of a speaker hampered by a poor or negative impression may tend to improve over time, thereby enhancing the possible acceptance or believability of the message. Since most of our public speaking activities are of a short-term nature, we should cultivate a positive image to take advantage of this short-term range of acceptance and believability. Commercial products that use national celebrities for spokespersons illustrate the significance of positive imagery in short-run communication endeavors.[4]

Finally, *initial decisions* that audiences reach about a speaker's image ("I really liked him—I thought he knew what he was talking about," or "I thought he was nothing more than a bull-throwing jerk") tend to be fairly resistant to change. That is, if you are viewed positively, then people will retain that positive image of you for an indefinite period; if you are seen negatively, you will suffer from this negative image indefinitely. That is why job and career counselors advise their clients that it is important to make a good first impression, for they know that this initial impression will be retained for a prolonged time.

All the various elements involved in effective speaking—from the selection of an appropriate and interesting topic through the effective delivery of the message—work together to create your image as a speaker. If one element slips, then it will take significant effort to turn your negative image into one that is positive. That is why you must approach each speaking situation with care, planning your speech very carefully from inception through actual delivery.

YOUR IMAGE AND ITS SOURCES

Having discussed the significance of the speaker's image and having briefly analyzed the major factors that create a positive or negative image, let us turn our attention to the sources of a speaker's credibility, examining both external and internal influences.

External Source Credibility Factors

Your image will be affected by factors that exist before you deliver your message. The most obvious external factor is information which is known about you before you speak ("I've heard that she's an excellent speaker," or "Bob told me that this guy'll bore you to tears"), whether or not that information is accurate.

You have met at least one person for the first time who has responded to your greeting by saying, "Ohhh, I've heard a lot about you!" At that point, you probably wanted to know exactly what that person had heard about you—was it good or bad? This same phenomenon exists in public speaking situations. Your reputation will precede you and will influence the reaction that your audience will have to you and to your message. Unfortunately, there is not a thing you can do about this fact, because you have no idea (1) what your "reputation" is with the various members of your audience, (2) what information (or lack of it) your reputation is based upon, and (3) whether that information and resultant reputation are accurate, partially true, or completely untrue. Now you know why major political figures are so concerned about their image, for they realize that this image will precede them, coloring the reactions that people have to them and their messages.

You might feel that being unknown to an audience will make these external factors irrelevant. However, human nature refuses to operate in a vacuum. Since people refuse to function in a situation without information (who you are, what you are like, and so on), they will provide that information themselves, largely through the use of stereotypes. It is through stereotyping that we supposedly know that all Englishmen wear hats and carry umbrellas; all Italians are great lovers; all Mexicans are lazy; all Germans are stern and autocratic; and all Jews have plenty of money.

As you can see, many stereotypes are racist and pernicious, so far from the truth that they severely damage the person stereotyped. This problem was noted by Professor Ayad Al-Qazzaz: "Stereotypes deal with category, thus overlooking the difference found among people with regard to a trait. They are erroneous, or half-truths, rather than accurate statements about the reality to which they refer."[5]

For years, women were stereotyped by the broadcast industry as having high and unpleasant nasal-quality voices, thereby making them unsuitable radio and television announcers and newscasters. People with high foreheads were categorized as intelligent "eggheads," and people who wore glasses were scholarly and bookish. We stereotype all football players as stupid, all doctors as rich and prone to play golf on Wednesdays, and all people with red hair as having quick tempers.

If you look at any stereotype individually, it is easy to find several people who do not fit the generalized mold. However, these stereotypes continue to exist, and they will confront you as an unknown speaker before an audience. You may be stereotyped by your profession or occupation; your perceived status; your physical appearance; your walk to the podium; and your vocal quality—the sound of your voice.

Of course, one of the greatest stereotypes is that of sex. You will be received somewhat differently depending upon your sex, and quick judgments will be made concerning you and your speech topic because of your sex.

Like your prespeech reputation, there is little that you can do about such stereotypes before the fact. Since you cannot change people's opinions before meeting them, you must wait until you speak to counter any erroneous impressions that may be held about you. As a professor of speech communication, I encounter this difficulty all the time ("You teach speech! I'll have to keep my mouth shut around you!"), and I find myself spending a great deal of time convincing people that I am a regular person, regardless of their preconceptions about speech teachers.[6]

Other external factors bear upon your speaking image (who

introduces you to speak; the mood the audience happens to be in; and the occasion upon which you speak), but your prior reputation and stereotypes about you are the most significant in establishing external source credibility.

Internal Source Credibility Factors

Once you have begun a speech, your image is affected by everything that goes into the makeup of that speech, and it is here that the factors of trustworthiness, competence, and dynamism come into play. Your speech topic, how it is organized, how it is worded, how it is delivered, and all other such items create internal speaker credibility, and that is why beginning speakers are constantly admonished to practice, practice, practice. You want to have a well-controlled presentation that will foster the most positive image possible.

Such a positive reaction to your speech can offset negative prespeech images (remember the difficulties I face as a speech teacher), but your task obviously is much more difficult. The more concrete your prespeech image is, the harder it will be to change that image during the course of one speech. That is why political campaigners and commercial advertisers (closely related animals, I might add) work with "campaigns," not just with one-shot communication attempts. To counter negative images requires a well-thought-out and lengthy effort; one sixty-second commercial will not do the job.

You do not have to be concerned about campaigns unless you decide to run for elective office. In most of your speaking situations, you will find that a well-planned, well-organized, and well-delivered speech will create the type of positive image you wish to have. In short, you possess the capability to create a positive, effective image as a communicator—if you are willing to work to create that image.

TIPS TO ENHANCE YOUR IMAGE

Since a positive speaking image is created by a combination of the various factors involved in effective speaking, the communication process as a whole must be seen as image producing.

However, ten tips should be considered if you want to have your audience see you in the most favorable light:

1. Select a topic that will be interesting and relevant to your audience. Do not pick a topic simply because it pleases you. Your audience must be your primary consideration in topic selection.

2. Select a topic that you can handle comfortably. Do not go over your head in trying to deal with materials or information with which you are not conversant, or you may end up looking like a fool.

3. Painstakingly organize your speech so that it makes logical sense to the listener. Do not use the stream-of-consciousness approach of throwing things together arbitrarily. You must have a definite method of organization.

4. Dress appropriately for your audience by wearing clothes that will be acceptable to them. Do not overdress or underdress. Remember, people make quick judgments about others based on the way they look.

5. If you have the power to do so, select an individual to introduce you who is held in high esteem by the audience. Believe it or not, that individual's image, good or bad, will rub off on you, affecting your image and the reaction to your speech.

6. Upon being introduced, walk directly and confidently to the podium. Avoid the extremes of approaching the podium as if you were going to your death or bounding up as if you were about to lead the group in jumping-jacks. People study a speaker's approach to the podium, so remember that you are on stage before you actually begin to speak.

7. Maintain a solid, well-balanced stance throughout your presentation. Do not lean on or over the podium. You must balance your need for being physically relaxed with the need to maintain control over your audience.

8. Establish and maintain direct eye contact with your audience. Do not look at the ceiling or the tops of your shoes. Direct eye contact tells your audience, "Keep listening to me. I've prepared this speech just for you."

9. Deliver your speech in a volume that will allow everyone to hear you easily. You do not want to make your audience strain to hear you, nor do you want to blow them out of the room by being too loud.

10. Deliver your speech enthusiastically, remembering that audiences prefer speakers who exhibit dynamic qualities. Of course, this delivery characteristic should not be taken to extremes, for the speaker who is too animated distracts the audience from the message and looks quite foolish.

Perhaps no other variable related to communication has been studied more than the speaker's image or credibility. It is very important in determining whether you and your message will be accepted or rejected by your audience. If you wish to create the most positive image possible, then work diligently at developing those speaking qualities which will enhance your image.

Notes

Chapter 5

Selling Yourself

1. For example, see Aristotle, *The Art of Rhetoric,* translated from the Greek by Lane Cooper (New York: Appleton-Century-Crofts, 1932).

2. The interrelationship between politics and images was explored most vigorously by Joe McGinniss, *The Selling of the President, 1968* (New York: Trident Press, 1969).

3. Interesting research findings concerning communicator credibility are noted by Marvin Karlins and Herbert I. Abelson, *Persuasion: How Opinions and Attitudes Are Changed,* 2d ed. (New York: Springer, 1970), pp. 108–32.

4. It is not by accident that Joe Namath has served as the commercial spokesman for popcorn poppers and pantyhose, or that veteran actor Jimmy Stewart was selected to represent Firestone Tire and Rubber Company.

5. Quoted by Jack G. Shaheen in *The Link* (April/May 1980), p. 1.

6. I often begin a speech by saying, "I wish to congratulate this audience for having the courage to listen to a speech teacher." I have found that this loosens up the audience by showing them I was not going to articulate a series of bird calls.

6

Delivering Your Message

All of us know how important effective delivery is in public speaking—especially when we recall speakers whose delivery left a great deal to be desired. Nothing can so devastate the impact of any speech as poor delivery; the finest topic, most arduous research, and most meticulous organization can be ruined if a speaker fails to present a message effectively.

Many centuries ago, the great Greek orator and statesman Demosthenes was asked to list the three most important elements for effective public speaking, and he answered, "Delivery, delivery, delivery." While his answer might be a bit exaggerated, it does indicate the significance of delivery to the oral communication process. The delivery of your speech, or the combined physical and verbal elements that transmit your message to your listeners, can make or break the impact of your presentation. Just as a baseball pitcher must have an effective delivery to be consistent, so too does the success of a public speaker depend upon delivery, for it is the element of public speaking that is most noticeable to the audience.

Overall, as a speaker you want to develop a delivery style that adds positively to the presentation of your message, facilitating the transmission of your message to your audience. The clarity of your message and how it is understood (or misunderstood) depends greatly upon the quality of your speaking delivery. However, since all speakers must contend with stagefright and with the extra levels of energy created by stagefright, much of this heightened energy level is translated into various delivery quirks, many of which are negative. At a minimum, you do not want your delivery qualities to detract from your message by calling undue attention to themselves. This chapter is designed to acquaint you with the major elements of effective public speaking delivery and to indicate those typical problems that ought to be avoided.

PHYSICAL ELEMENTS OF DELIVERY

When we mention your speaking delivery, we refer to both your physical and verbal qualities as a speaker. Yet to examine this important area vividly, those two component areas have been separated for easier scrutiny. Within this section, five major physical elements of delivery will be explored: eye contact, gestures, facial expression, physical posture, and movement.

Eye Contact

Every public speaking teacher you will ever meet will tell you it is essential to establish and maintain direct eye contact with your audience. This is one of the most sound pieces of advice you can receive as a public speaker. By looking at your audience (not down at your shoes or at the ceiling or out a window), you will be able to see their reactions to your message. Does your audience understand what you are saying, or are they confused? Do they agree with your position, or do they disagree? Are they happy, angry, or indifferent? You can't answer any of those questions without looking at your audience to gauge their reactions to your message.

When we examined the communication process in chapter 2, we noted that an important part of that process was feedback, the reactions of the audience to you and your message. Since most of this feedback is nonverbal, you must look at your audience to see if they understand your message, are angered or pleased by it, interested or bored. Only by looking at your audience can you see if your listeners are yawning, peering intently at you (possibly because they aren't certain of what you're saying), looking around aimlessly (showing they have lost interest in your message), and so on. Maintaining direct eye contact with your audience is crucial if you are to pick up these important nonverbal cues.

Eye contact serves at least one other important purpose: it shows the audience that you are interested in them, that you want them to listen to your message. Direct eye contact says, in effect, "Hey, listen to me. What I'm saying is of importance to *you.*" Now, consider the impact of the speaker who fails to look at the audience. Instead of showing interest in that audience, the lack of eye contact shows disinterest, and audiences will not pay attention to a speaker who exhibits such disinterest. You must establish direct eye contact at the start of your speech and maintain it all the way through.

Sometime during your life you may have expressed concern about looking directly at your audience ("I can't do it. All those eyes will be looking back at me!!"). Perhaps you were advised that you could give the impression of eye contact by merely "looking over the heads of the audience." That advice presumes that the people in your audience are stupid, which they are not. If you attempt to cheat on eye contact by looking over the heads of your audience, you will find your listeners turning around, trying to figure out what it is at the back of the room that you find so interesting that you must look at it instead of them. Audiences know when a speaker is looking just over the tops of their heads; you cannot cheat on eye contact in this manner. Instead of remembering the content of your message, your audience will remember only that you stared at the back of the room during the delivery of your speech.

In maintaining this desired eye contact, you certainly do not want to stare weirdly at your audience, nor is it necessary that you look directly at every member of your audience sometime during your speech. (If you had one hundred people in your audience, that would be nearly impossible to accomplish). You do not have to look at each person in your audience, but you should give the impression that you have done so. As you begin your speech, pick out three people—one seated to your right, one to your left, and one directly in the center of your audience —and speak to them. Concentrate upon these three people as you speak, focusing your eye contact primarily upon them. Your peripheral vision will give the impression that you have looked at nearly everyone, while, in fact, you have looked at three. Not only will this help you deal with the issue of eye contact, but it also helps to combat stagefright. After all, you're not speaking to one hundred people, you're only speaking to three!

Looking directly at an audience might seem frightening if you've never given a public speech before, but remember: the members of your audience are pulling for you; they want you to succeed. Look at them and feel and see the positive reactions they give you. Take advantage of this most pleasant kind of feedback. Not only will direct eye contact with your audience make you feel better and more relaxed, it will aid the impact of your presentation immeasurably.[1]

Gestures

All people use their hands while speaking. If you watch people engaged in casual conversation, you will note that hands are used to underscore expression, to add emphasis to what is said verbally. So, too, do public speakers use their hands, for these gestures add to the intensity and dynamism of public discourse. Teachers, ministers, politicians—all use their hands to gesture while speaking.

You use your hands when you talk, even though you probably are not aware of it. Were you to sit on your hands while chatting with someone, you quickly would feel uncomfortable, for you would realize that something was wrong—your hands weren't free to help you express yourself. You have used your hands in past public speaking situations, but your primary concern over message transmission to your audience made you unaware of your hand usage in these situations as well.

There is a great difference between an informal chat with a friend and a public speech: the degree of formality that accompanies any public presentation. With that formality goes a degree of pressure, and that pressure often is manifested in stagefright. Significantly, speakers often use their hands to eliminate the extra energy created by stagefright, and it is not unusual to see speakers crack their knuckles, play with parts of their clothing (as Johnny Carson fiddles with his tie during his opening monologue), twist their fingers in their hair (women), jingle coins and keys in their pocket (men), and fondle jewelry, such as rings, watches, or bracelets. Most of the time, these speakers are totally unaware of what their hands are doing, because their attention is focused upon the transmission of their message.

To use your hands effectively, you must always remain aware of what your hands are doing. This means that you will have to concentrate upon your hand movements, remembering what kinds of actions are to be avoided because they distract the audience from your message. You do not have to rehearse what your hands should do, for they will naturally move in ways consistent with your message, but you must be certain that your hands do not work against the effective oral presentation of your message.[2]

One final thought about hand gestures pertains primarily to men. Perhaps you were told years ago that it is improper or slovenly to slip one hand into your pants pocket while speaking. That simply is not true. There is nothing wrong with having one hand in your pocket, for it will help to relax you and will create a positive attitude of conversational informality. However, you should not jingle the contents of this pocket (I often refer to this as the reindeer-on-the-roof syndrome), nor should you tuck both hands away. One hand, casually placed in your pocket, is most acceptable.

Your hands are most helpful in underscoring expression, so let them work for you. Don't hide them behind your back, or trap them on or under the podium. Don't clasp your arms or hands together. Let your hands be free to gesture, and the effectiveness of your delivery will be enhanced substantially.

Facial Expression

Some people teach that a speaker has to manipulate the face a great deal while speaking to make the facial expression conform to the content of the message. Thus, the speaker is told to smile when delivering a happy message, frown when the message is sad, etc. This is completely unnecessary, for researchers such as Paul Ekman have documented the existence of the "facial affect program," meaning that emotional states within us tend to trigger a corresponding appropriate configuration of our facial muscular movements. We smile when we express a happy thought or frown when we have a sad thought, and we do all of this without having to think about it. Therefore, you do not have to manipulate your face like a circus clown; your facial expressions will naturally appear without your having to be concerned about this physical delivery element.

Physical Posture

At all times, you should effect a poised and direct posture as you speak, not slouching or leaning or standing stiff like a storefront mannequin. Having such a straightforward yet relaxed posture serves you in two ways. First, it helps you to feel physically at ease while you speak. If you stand squarely on both feet, you will not tire as quickly as those speakers who place most of their weight on but one leg. Just like golfers who want to evenly distribute their weight in teeing-off, so should public speakers distribute their weight for maximum comfort while speaking.

Besides helping you to relax, proper posture creates a positive impression in the eyes of your audience. The speaker who stands tall and direct is looked upon with greater favor than the speaker who slouches or leans on the podium. Speaker credibility is important in selling your message, and proper posture will help you achieve that goal.

Movement

It is not unusual to see a speaker try to eliminate nervous energy through an excessive amount of movement while speaking. Often creating a moving target, the speaker will pace back and forth, run circles around the podium, or dash toward and back from the audience. Of course, this much movement is horribly distracting, causing the audience to concentrate upon this action while forgetting to listen to the speaker's message. On the other hand, most people find it difficult to stay in one spot while delivering a speech (unless, of course, there is a stationary microphone that prohibits movement altogether). So, what should you do?

As a speaker, you need to be relaxed while speaking, so some movement is necessary. This also will provide visual relaxation for your audience, as it is tiring to concentrate upon one figure in one spot. Occasional movements of about two steps from one side to another will prove to be beneficial to both you and your audience. If, however, you fear that once you start moving you'll become that dreaded "moving target," take a tip from the fashion magazines and stand like a model with one foot slightly in front of the other. By occasionally shifting weight forward and then backward, you will be able to maintain your physical ease while creating the appearance of movement. Remember that some movement is both necessary and good; too much movement is distracting and harmful to effective communication.

VERBAL ELEMENTS OF DELIVERY

While the physical elements of delivery convey important visual messages to your audience, three main verbal delivery elements will affect their auditory senses. To be an effective speaker, you need to be concerned with clarity, fluency, and vocal modulators.

Clarity

To help your audience hear and understand your message, you must speak in a clear voice. You have heard speakers who did not have vocal clarity—they spoke "with cotton in their mouths," or ran their words together so that the message was very difficult to understand. Such problems can be solved if you take the time to deal with them.

First, clear articulation is necessary if you are to make each word understandable to your audience. Besides practicing at home in your leisure time, you should "loosen up" your articulators (the tongue, teeth, and lips) before each speech you deliver. Take a couple of minutes to manipulate your facial muscles by opening your mouth as widely as possible, by smiling extravagantly, and by moving your lower jaw up and down very quickly. After doing those facial exercises, practice a tongue twister several times, such as "red blood, blue blood," to develop articulatory precision. Those few minutes spent on such activities before you speak will enhance your verbal clarity.

You will find it useful to drink a small quantity of liquid before speaking. This rinses the mouth and throat, making it easier and more pleasant to speak. If possible, make that liquid water or black coffee. Do not consume soda pop, because that will make your mouth feel sticky and make precise articulation more difficult. Similarly, milk, especially chocolate milk, should be avoided. Contrary to a popular theory, you ought to avoid alcoholic beverages, for they might make your mouth so loose that you'll say things you had not intended to say.[3]

Finally, be careful about the way you put words together while speaking. Avoid using the same sound at the end of one word and at the beginning of the next word ("The four*th th*eory . . ."). Running those sounds together makes it difficult for the audience to understand the words you have used, and it is difficult for you to clearly differentiate the words without swallowing your tongue.

Fluency

If there is one problem that affects most speakers' verbal deliveries it is a lack of fluency, the smooth rolling of words one after another throughout a speech. Most people are nonfluent public communicators, chopping up their presentations with such sounds as "ahhh," "ummm," and "errr." Those sounds do not indicate poor thoughts or low intelligence, nor do they detract from the worth of the content of the speech. Instead, those "vocalized pauses" distract the audience from the message. Once the audience becomes aware of the many vocalized pauses in your speech, they'll concentrate upon those sounds and not upon your message. At that point you have, in effect, lost your audience. They're listening to your choppy delivery rather than what you are saying.

You have heard speakers who are nonfluent, and you know that this lack of fluency can drive an audience to wish that they were somewhere else instead of suffering through that presentation. Why do speakers say "ahhh," "ummm," and "errr?" Primarily, we use those sounds to buy time. Having just finished one thought, we need to think about what we intend to say next, and we create the necessary time with a vocalized pause. Sometimes, speakers will utter actual words to fill in this gap, and it is not unusual to hear "you know," "okay," and "now" used to link thoughts together. All such unnecessary sounds and words distract audiences from your message; they should be eliminated (or at least reduced) from your normal speaking repertoire.

Instead of using vocalized pauses when you're thinking of what to say next, use a silent pause instead. This pause will be brief, and silence literally is golden in comparison with "ahhh," "ummm," and "errr." You do not have to fill every second of your speech with some sort of sound, so when you must take a moment to collect your thoughts, pause *silently*. Your audience will appreciate it, and your message will not be hampered.

The only way to reduce or eliminate needless sounds is to concentrate upon what you're saying. There is no magic cure for vocalized pauses. You must think about what you're saying before you say it, trying to minimize unnecessary sounds and words. You might also want to practice a technique I call "go-go speaking":

1. Have a friend make a list of six or seven unrelated nouns.

2. Have your friend choose one of those words. Immediately begin speaking about that word, taking little or no time to think or pause.

3. As you are speaking, your friend should interrupt, giving you another word to speak about.

4. With each new word, you are to stop talking about the preceding word and immediately begin to speak about the new word. This exercise can be completed within two or three minutes, and if you repeat this exercise often, you'll find that your speaking fluency will be improved.

Go-Go Speaking List
- Christmas Tree
- Aluminum Foil
- Catcher's Mitt
- Deodorant
- Lawnmower
- Calendar Watch

The Vocal Modulators

The final verbal element of delivery we will examine is the use of the vocal modulators—rate, pitch, and volume, all of which are important to effective public speakers.

It is fairly obvious that you want to speak at a delivery rate that is comfortable for both you and your audience. Generally, an acceptable rate of delivery is 150 to 175 words per minute, a rate which allows your audience to keep pace with your thoughts as you speak. However, one of the most prevalent reactions to stage fright is for the speaker to talk at a much faster delivery rate than normal, to hit 250 or 300 words per minute. At that speed, many audience members cannot keep up, and they'll miss a great deal of what you say.

If you practice your speeches at home (highly recommended, but not in front of a mirror because you'll feel silly and self-conscious), you may find that it takes twelve minutes to deliver your material. In front of an audience, however, it would not be unusual to have that speech take only eight or nine minutes to deliver. Why? Stagefright. Hyperactivity caused by stage-fright tends to make speakers deliver their speeches at a much faster rate in public than that at home, and speakers who talk "a blue streak" leave their audiences gasping for air.

To minimize the chances of speaking too rapidly, take a deep breath just before beginning your speech. This will help you to relax so that you won't begin at a mind-bending speed, and once you begin speaking at such a controlled rate, you'll find it is much easier to modify your delivery rate throughout the entire presentation. Remember to adjust your rate of delivery so that it is comfortable both to you and to your audience and does not detract from the content of your speech.

Much like your delivery rate, the pitch of your voice (its high and low sounds) is an important element of effective delivery. You have a normal pitch range when you speak, and it is something that you do not think about during routine daily conversations. However, in public speaking situations it is not unusual to find speakers talking at an abnormally high pitch because of the extra energy and excitement generated by stage-fright. If you speak at an abnormal pitch height for any sub-stantial length of time, you'll become hoarse because of the unusual strain placed upon your vocal cords.

To prevent this from happening, a deep breath at the start of your speech will relax your vocal folds, and a drink of cool water will help matters even more. Then, throughout the entire presentation of your speech, you should concentrate upon speaking at your normal pitch height, refraining from such actions as shouting out your speech (a problem that affects Senator Edward Kennedy, for example). If you retain your normal pitch as a public speaker, a long presentation will not be taxing to your voice and will not cause your vocal quality to deteriorate.

Your vocal quality will also be aided by the final vocal modulator, volume. Of course, you should speak at a volume that allows everyone in the audience to hear you easily. You have to speak more loudly in larger rooms than in smaller ones, and you have to increase your volume if there are noise problems in the surrounding environment (airplanes overhead or a lawn mower being operated outside the meeting room). You do not want to whisper, nor do you want to shout. Your volume must be appropriate to the physical layout and audience arrangement of each particular speaking occasion.

In large assembly halls, you may be provided with a microphone, and the appropriate volume will be created mechanically. However, you should remember to speak *across* the microphone, not directly into it. This will prevent a "breathy" sound and it also will keep you from spitting into the mike. If you will be using a microphone, try to practice with it if for just a few seconds so that you'll be comfortable using it.

TWO PROBLEM AREAS: THE PODIUM AND NOTES

Regardless of the speaking situation or purpose, most speakers are beset by problems caused by the speaker's podium and the note materials used to organize their speeches. This section will provide you with several suggestions for dealing with those problem areas.

The podium (or lectern or speaker's stand) is designed to give you a place to put your notes so that you can refer to them easily while still maintaining good direct eye contact with your audience. As a teacher of public communication, I do not like to see speakers use a podium, because it physically separates them from their audiences. Instead, I prefer to see speakers stand directly and clearly in front of their audiences, holding their notes in one hand while gesturing with the other. Still, I realize that many people find it difficult to do this, and situations involving a stationary podium microphone demand that the podium be used. If you decide to use a podium, be careful not to commit any of the five cardinal abuses of many podium-users:

1. Beating on the podium. Some speakers carry on as if the podium were their greatest enemy, banging fists against the poor object to emphasize each important point. Physically abusing the podium only creates a visual and auditory distraction.

2. Holding onto the podium. Just as the character Linus in the "Peanuts" comic strip constantly carries a blanket with him for security, many public speakers use the podium as a security blanket. In fact, many speakers put a "death grip" on the podium, causing the blood to drain from their knuckles as they hold on for dear life. Not only does this not solve the nervousness caused by stagefright, it also eliminates the use of hand gestures, an important part of effective oral communication.

3. Lying on the podium. For some reason, some speakers decide to rest their arms from the elbows down on the podium, occasionally standing up straight at various points within their speeches. This jack-in-the-box movement is distracting, and poor posture harms the speaker's image.

4. Leaning over the podium. When you're behind the podium, you become aware immediately that there is a physical block between you and your audience. Some speakers try to overcome this block by leaning over the podium, looking almost as if they are about to climb over it and leap into the audience's laps. As a result, the speaker's posture is poor, gestures are nonexistent, and the audience is taken aback by the speaker's sloppy appearance.

5. Running to and from the podium. A most visually-irritating sight is the speaker who appears to play hide-and-seek by

darting out from behind the podium and then running back to its safety over and over again. There is, of course, nothing for any public speaker to fear, so this hide-and-seek game is completely unnecessary. Besides, the podium doesn't really provide you with any security anyway. If you wish to use the podium, then use it; if you choose not to use the podium, then don't use it—but you cannot have it both ways.

Overall, please remember that the podium exists only to provide you with a convenient device to hold your notes. It should not be used in a way which hampers effective communication. As you become more skilled as a public speaker, you will find that you need the podium less and less—and you will communicate more effectively and more directly without it.

The second major problem confronting most speakers is the use of notes. Should notes be used? What kind? How should they be used while speaking? If you are a relative novice, you will find that note materials can help you to overcome even the most severe form of stagefright, memory loss. However, notes can also present problems. Some speakers use so many notes that the podium is virtually cluttered with scraps of paper. The more notes you have, the greater the tendency for you to read your speech to the audience. There is a great difference between public speaking and public reading, with the latter being much more boring and tiring, primarily because few people can read well aloud. However, at the first inkling of nervousness, many speakers dive into their notes, reading to a bored audience without any gestures, movement, eye contact, or dynamism.

To use notes productively, consider the following suggestions:

1. Use as few notes as possible, trying to work from an outline of the major points you wish to make.

2. Put your notes on note cards (preferably the four by six inch size) instead of using regular sheets of paper. The note cards will force you to limit the amount of information you

carry, and they are less clumsy and bulky than notebook paper.

3. Type your notes or record them in ink. Notes written in pencil can easily be smudged by sweaty hands.

4. Number your note cards so that they can be kept in proper order, and write or type on only one side of each note card to minimize confusion as to how they should be arranged.

5. Finally, try to use your notes as discreetly as possible. Refrain from tapping them on the podium or tying up both your hands with them so that you cannot gesture.

As with the podium, notes should be used to facilitate effective communication, not block it. Notes can help you present your message to your audience; they must not be allowed to detract from your presentation.

TYPES OF DELIVERY

In speaking before a group, you generally have a choice of three possible delivery types: speaking from memorization, speaking from manuscript, or speaking extemporaneously.[4] Each delivery type has advantages and disadvantages.

Speaking from Memorization

The most difficult delivery style is to speak from memory, although it does seem to have its appeal. All the speaker must do is write a speech and then memorize it word for word. However, this presents several problems for the speaker. First, a lengthy speech is difficult to memorize—as every actor can attest. Second, speech delivery is stilted, because the speaker is more concerned with remembering "what comes next" than with communicating effectively with the audience. Third, there is complete disaster when the speaker forgets what comes next, when there is a block in the memorization pattern. This block might last only a few seconds, but to the speaker it seems like an eternity. Speaking from memory is not a good idea for most speakers.

Speaking from Manuscript

Using a manuscript is much like speaking from memory, except that the speech is not memorized. Instead, the speech is written out and then read to the audience exactly as written. Major political figures use this delivery type (they use tele-prompters when making televised addresses) to be absolutely certain of what they say. Like speaking from memory, manu-script speaking has more disadvantages than advantages for most speakers. First, few people can read a speech well. They tend to suffer from vocal flatness—they have little vocal expres-siveness and color. Second, reading a speech eliminates eye contact, most gestures, and most physical movement. Finally, a manuscript speech ties a speaker to what has been written, with no flexibility to change it if the audience or speaking situation so warrants. In short, manuscript speaking does not promote effective oral communication.

Speaking Extemporaneously

The most natural and dynamic delivery type is to speak extem-poraneously. In this style, the speaker relies on only a few notes and probably an outline. The words used to connect these major thoughts are extemporized as the speech is delivered. Obviously, this adds a great deal of dynamism and vivacity to the speaker's presentation, making the speech come alive as it is presented. This delivery style might appear to be frightening, because you don't know exactly what you are going to say before you speak. However, if you have researched your topic well and if you have practiced your speech several times, then you have nothing to fear. You *know* what you want to say, and your outlined notes are there to help you along. Extemporane-ous speaking does not mean that you are speaking "cold"; it means that you are speaking with a sense of liveliness and creativity that will be appreciated by your audience.

If you are a novice speaker, memorizing a speech or reading it might be seductive to you. But remember what it has been like when you've been a member of an audience. Did you enjoy the noncommunicative nature of a memorized speech? Did you enjoy the boredom generated by a manuscript speech? Your own experiences as an audience member should convince you that the best speakers, the ones you most enjoy, are the ones who speak extemporaneously.

USING AUDIO-VISUAL AIDS

There are times in presenting information when it is quite helpful to use audio-visual materials to augment what you say in your speech. Some topics are so intricate or difficult that the audience needs to see or hear materials which help to clarify what is said by the speaker. For example, an informative presentation about the workings of the internal combustion engine might be confusing unless the speaker complements the presentation with diagrams or a model to show how the engine works. Similarly, a television weather reporter would be horribly hamstrung without a large map of the United States for showing the audience how the various high and low pressure systems were moving across the country. Audio-visual materials can clarify otherwise confusing information.

In addition, audio-visual materials serve to increase audience recall of the information presented within a speech. Research indicates that a speech using visual aids heightens the long-term recall of information dramatically: only 10 percent of a speech's information is recalled three days after the speech is given, but that recall rate can be increased to 65 percent when the speech is augmented by visual aids.[5] So, if you want your audience to remember your message and to recall more details of your message for a longer time, then add audio-visual materials to your presentation.

Unfortunately, many speakers do not effectively use these materials, especially visual aids. So, before you add audio-visual materials to your speech, take a moment to read the following checklist, making certain that all your speech materials are used in a way which enhances oral communication.

1. All visual materials must be clearly seen by your audience, and all audio materials must be clearly heard. You must plan your audio-visual aids according to the size of the room in which you will speak as well as the probable size of the audience.

2. All visual materials must be easily understood by your audience. Too many speakers clutter their visuals with too much information, making their charts and graphs a hodge-podge of confusion.

3. Audio-visual materials should be limited in number. You should use only those materials which are essential to the effective presentation of your message. Some speakers are so enamored of visual aids that they clutter their speeches with them, creating communication overload. Too many visuals are just as ineffective as a speech that needs visuals but does not have them.

4. When using visual aids, you must be certain that you do not block the audience's view of them, or turn your attention away from the audience toward your visual aid. It is easy for you to be distracted by your own visual materials (and you will see many speakers talking to their visuals and not to their audience), but you must remember that your primary attention should be directed toward the members of your audience.

5. Finally, you must know before your speech exactly how your audio-visual materials are going to be placed before your audience. Will you hold your chart or have it placed on a tripod device? Will there be a table to hold your tape recorder? Will you use a pointer while referring to your chart or graph? Those are the kinds of questions that you must resolve long before the time for your speech. If you assume that a tripod, or a table, or a pointer will be available for your use, you might be horribly surprised to discover that it is not. You must be prepared before your speech, and you cannot assume that everything you need will be provided for you.

A number of materials of both an audio and visual nature might be useful in your speeches. Figure 6.1 delineates the main types of audio-visual aids available and the major advantages and disadvantages of each aid. Audio-visual aids can add a dynamic and interesting dimension to your public speeches if you use them well.

Fig. 6.1. AUDIO-VISUAL AIDS

AID	ADVANTAGES	DISADVANTAGES
Nonprojected Aids		
1. Chalkboard	Nice when advanced preparation is not feasible.	Speaker must turn away from audience to use. Usually sloppy.
2. Posters	Good for color drawings. Can be preserved.	Clumsy and bulky.
3. Pictures	Good substitute for the real thing.	Hard to see if audience is big. Can be expensive.
4. Flipchart	Easy to use. Can be consulted several times during presentation.	Difficult to transport.
5. Models	Reduces or enlarges actual object.	Expensive and time-consuming to prepare.
6. Mock-ups	Almost as good as the real thing.	Usually expensive.
7. Graphs/Charts	Good for showing flow, trends, quantities, comparisons.	Time-consuming to prepare.
8. Handouts	Can be saved and used by audience. Can aid while talking.	Can distract if used while talking. Must have one for everyone.

Fig. 6.1.—*Continued*

AID	ADVANTAGES	DISADVANTAGES

Nonprojected Aids

9. Volunteers	Audience involvement.	Must be "trained."
10. Tape recordings	Complements other aids where sound is important.	Time-consuming preparation. Rehearsal needed.

Projected Aids

1. Overhead projector	Speaker can face audience while using. Room can be lit. Inexpensive. Can be written on during speech.	Picture must have carbon content.
2. Opaque projector	Projects pictures directly. No preparation necessary.	Must darken room. Bulky, obstructs view.
3. Slide projector	Operates easily. Can face audience. Can be remote controlled. Can preserve.	Must plan well ahead—develop, organized slides. Must darken room.
4. Videotape	Useful when motion is needed. Easy to refer to.	Expensive. Bulky to handle. Hard to use with large audience.
5. Film	Useful when relevant and professionally done.	Must compete with film. Must darken room.

Notes

Chapter 6

Delivering Your Message

1. During the past two decades, researchers in communication, psychology, and sociology have conducted numerous studies about the use and importance of eye contact. In terms of non-verbal communication, eye contact (or EC as the researchers refer to it) may be the most important variable in face-to-face communication encounters.

2. Public speakers during the latter part of the nineteenth century were influenced by the study of "elocution," the notion that all physical movement and vocal inflection had to be carefully controlled because each had its own inherent interpretation. See G. P. Mohrmann, "The Language of Nature and Elocutionary Theory," *Quarterly Journal of Speech,* 70 (April 1966), pp. 116–24.

3. The public speaker should remember Thoreau's advice in *Walden:* "Water is the only drink for a wise man."

4. Some professional groups also utilize a delivery type called "impromptu speaking," wherein a speaker is given a topic and is asked to speak on that topic without any kind of preparation. Obviously, impromptu speaking is not something for the novice public speaker.

5. R. Benschofter in Robert Haakenson, *Effective Communication for Engineers,* (New York: McGraw-Hill, 1974), p. 66.

7

What Should You Do Next Time?

As you will discover, no speech ever goes exactly as planned, and no speech ever has the exact impact anticipated by the speaker. In fact, few speakers emerge from a speaking situation completely happy, for they tend to be more aware of what went wrong rather than what went right. Therefore, you should not be surprised to feel a bit letdown after your speech, to think, "I could have done better." Yes, you could have done better, and you *will* do better, because there is one certainty about public speaking: there is always room for improvement.

After each speech, you should take some time to think about it. Think about your prespeech preparation and practice as well as your delivery during the speech itself. To aid in this assessment, use the following checklist to organize your thoughts:

EVALUATING YOUR SPEECH

1. Preparation. Did I select a topic that was pertinent to my audience, to me, and to the speaking occasion? Did I select a topic that was of interest to my audience and to me? Did I study my audience beforehand?

2. Research. Did I consider everything that I knew about the topic in planning my speech? Did I secure necessary outside research materials to support the main points? Did I use my research time effectively in gathering all necessary materials? Did I record my research information clearly, allowing me to decipher what I had written long after it was recorded?

3. Organization. Did I carefully consider the types of organizational structures which might be appropriate to my speech? Did I select the final organizational pattern upon the issues of topic and audience needs? Did I revamp and reorganize my material to make it clear, concise, and logical? Did the overall organization of information make sense to my audience? Was the audience able to follow the pattern of my speech?

4. Practice. Did I practice my speech aloud at least twice? Did I critically evaluate my practice sessions, modifying content and delivery as appropriate? Did I go to my speaking situation feeling that I was fully prepared to speak?

5. Delivery. Did I strike a direct and confident pose as I spoke, establishing a conversational physical rapport with my audience? Did I use my body effectively as I spoke, gesturing and moving naturally and maintaining direct eye contact with my audience? If I used the podium, did I use it effectively? Was my vocal quality clear and crisp? Could everyone hear me easily, and did they find my vocal quality pleasant and appropriate to my topic? Did I speak at an acceptable rate of delivery, and did I vary my vocal pitch and delivery rate to maintain audience attention and interest? If I used audio-visual aids, did I use them effectively?

6. Communication. Did I make my speech meaningful to my audience, especially the choice of words employed in my speech? Did I consider audience attitudes in preparing my speech, and did I pay attention to audience reactions during my speech? Did I use feedback during my speech to modify its structure and content to have a more direct impact upon my audience? Can I truly say that I effectively communicated my message to my audience?

Referring to the questions above will help you to develop a very comprehensive assessment of your speech performance. By examining your speech in this manner instead of the usual gut reaction ("It went fantastically" or "It was a bomb"), you will discover information which will help you in your next speaking engagement.

There is one thing that you must remember: the public speaker has the worst perception of how a speech went, whether it was successful, disastrous, or somewhere in between. Because *you* were the speaker and because it was *your* speech, you are so much involved in the resultant product that you are not really objective as your own speech evaluator. Most speakers tend to criticize their own efforts much too harshly, to overlook the positive elements while dwelling too heavily upon the problems they had (or think that they had). So, it is helpful to ask for a critique of your speech from one or two members of your audience. After all, they were the consumers of your speech, so their reactions ought to prove quite valuable in assessing the impact of your presentation. To simplify this process, you might ask these evaluators to respond to several of the questions included in the postspeech checklist in this chapter.

SOME FINAL THOUGHTS

Chances are that you are not a greatly experienced public speaker; otherwise you would not have bought this book. You may be exactly the person this book was written for: someone who has something of value to say, but who has, for one reason or another, developed a real fear of public speaking. Welcome to perhaps the largest club in the United States! As I told you at the start of this book, a national survey indicated that many people fear giving a speech more than they fear death. At this point you should realize that public speaking is nothing to fear, because

1. stagefright is a natural phenomenon.
2. stagefright affects all speakers.

3. stagefright can be controlled through preparation and practice.

4. stagefright is helpful, because it "keeps you on your toes," making your speeches more dynamic and interesting.

You have nothing to fear as a public speaker, because you are engaged in the most basic form of communication in human interaction. You have nothing to fear, because your own practice and preparation will cause you to succeed. You have nothing to fear, because your audiences are pulling for you; your audiences want you to do well. You have nothing to fear, because effective public speaking simply is the application of a method to the presentation of ideas in public discourse. If you will apply the methods and suggestions detailed in this book, you will do well as a public speaker. I not only *believe* that to be true, I guarantee it.

In looking at the gloomy situation caused by the Great Depression, President Franklin Roosevelt told the American people in 1933 that the only thing they had to fear was fear itself. The same can be said for the public speaker. There are no goblins in your audiences; the earth will not open to swallow you up. Your biggest obstacle to effective public speaking is your self-induced fear, and you have the power to overcome it. Use this book to control your fear; use it to allow yourself to become the kind of speaker you have always wanted to be. You can do it. You will do it. Then you can truly say that public speaking is one of the most exciting and exhilarating experiences you have had, and you will come to enjoy each and every public speaking situation as I do!

Index

111